NEW
SLOW
CITY

ALSO BY WILLIAM POWERS

Blue Clay People: Seasons on Africa's Fragile Edge

Whispering in the Giant's Ear:
A Frontline Chronicle from Bolivia's War on Globalization

Twelve by Twelve:
A One-Room Cabin Off the Grid and Beyond
the American Dream

NEW
SLOW
CITY

living
simply
in the
world's
fastest city

WILLIAM
POWERS

New World Library
Novato, California

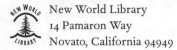 New World Library
14 Pamaron Way
Novato, California 94949

Cover and interior illustrations by Kyle Pierce, kylepierceillustration.com

Text design by Tona Pearce Myers

Library of Congress Cataloging-in-Publication Data is available.

First printing, November 2014
ISBN 978-1-60868-239-3
Printed in Canada on 100% postconsumer-waste recycled paper

 New World Library is proud to be a Gold Certified Environmentally Responsible Publisher. Publisher certification awarded by Green Press Initiative. www.greenpressinitiative.org

10 9 8 7 6 5 4 3 2 1

CONTENTS

PART 3. WINTER TO SPRING:
    Flight Paths

PREFACE

THIS BOOK ORIGINATED with a somewhat angry question. It came from a reader of *Twelve by Twelve: A One-Room Cabin Off the Grid and Beyond the American Dream*, my previous book about living in a twelve-foot-by-twelve-foot off-grid cabin in North Carolina. "It's easy," she wrote, "to find minimalism, joy, connection to nature, and abundant time in a shack in the woods. But how the hell are the rest of us supposed to stay sane in our busy modern lives?"

I received a hundred variations of this question in emails, after lectures, and during television and radio interviews about *Twelve by Twelve*.

I always answered by saying I *was* living 12 x 12 values... but in Queens, New York — the home to which I returned after my time in the cabin. But as each year passed, the reader's doubt increasingly became my own as overwork, material clutter, and the lack of contact with nature — "civilization," in short

— brought me to a point of extreme unhappiness in Queens. Eventually, I too doubted it was possible to live 12 x 12 in a city, and I felt an urgent need to decamp far from urban life.

Not so fast. As I reached this point, my newlywed wife, Melissa, was offered an excellent job that demanded we stay put in New York City, and I suddenly had no choice but to figure out how to take what I'd learned in the 12 x 12 — about the Leisure Ethic, connecting to nature, and living simply — and somehow make it work in the real-world context of a marriage and two careers.

In an attempt to do this, Melissa and I embarked on an experiment. We sold or gave away 80 percent of our stuff, left our 1,600-square-foot Queens townhouse, crossed the Williamsburg Bridge, and moved into a tiny rental: a 340-square-foot "micro-apartment" — roughly two 12 x 12s — on the fifth floor of a nineteenth-century walk-up in downtown Manhattan.

New Slow City is a memoir of that experience, in which we spent a year living the Leisure Ethic in a New York minute. It is an adventure into smart-city trends ranging from Slow Food and Slow Travel to technology fasting, urban sanctuaries, bodysurfing the Rockaways, and rooftop farming. Books like David Owen's *Green Metropolis* (on the eco-city), Carl Honoré's *In Praise of Slowness* (on the global Slow movement), and Alex Mitchell's *The Edible Balcony* (on urban agriculture) wonderfully capture specific facets of *New Slow City*, but this book aims for a more holistic, personal approach. Through the microcosm of one couple's quest to, as the *Twelve by Twelve* reader wrote, "find minimalism, joy, connection to nature, and abundant time," I examine what Urban Slow means, and what it feels like, in real terms. For us, it meant working less (I scaled back to a two-day workweek), having a light ecological footprint, and living in the present moment.

To protect their identities, some people's names and distinguishing details have been changed. Also, I've sometimes collapsed multiple conversations into one or telescoped chronology. I trust readers will forgive me for a little literary license to tighten the book's narrative in this true account of a year in New York.

Cities aren't the enemies of a centered life. Mindfulness arises from inside, after all, so what's needed, I came to discover, are the right questions and practices. Nor are cities the enemy of the environment. Because of New York's population density, the average New Yorker has one-third the carbon footprint of the average Vermonter. According to current population trends, the world in 2050 will swell to ten billion people — 70 percent of them urban — and their appetites will grow. Figuring out cities is vital.

It's urgent we begin to do so now. Gallup recently reported that 70 percent of American employees are either unhappy or disengaged at work. Anxiety levels among adolescents and adults are soaring, even compared to just two decades ago. One out of every four adults in America experiences some form of depression in the course of their lives. In Japan, they have a name for people who die from overworking: karoshi. Could we in the United States be tipping toward becoming a nation of karoshis? I, for one, became so stressed by constant work and the pace of city life that — before our Slow Year experiment — I found myself nearly a karoshi myself. I'm convinced that society must find a new equilibrium between the demands of business, the consumptive habits of society, and our own personal happiness.

[handwritten margin notes: "urbanization continues" and "die from overworking) karoshi"]

This great task begins with a pause.

We need space to ask the core questions, like: How do we find balance in a world that is changing more quickly than ever before in history? How do we overcome our culture's ingrained habits of too much clutter, total work, and permanent distraction? And is it possible for individuals, against the odds, to incubate a new urban culture that's slower, saner, and fit for the future?

PART I

SPRING TO SUMMER
The Natural City

1. VICTORY GARDEN

OUR MOVING VAN DASHES over the Williamsburg Bridge as we hurtle into Manhattan to start our Slow Year. My head is partway out the passenger window. Wind massages my scalp, the East River sparkles below, and the New York skyline swells against a metallic blue sky. The Empire State Building towers haughtily over everything until it's hidden by a cluster of approaching Alphabet City high-rises. I'm flush with excitement — *Manhattan! Our new life!* — as Jack, our overweight, chain-smoking van driver, floors it.

"Bill?" my wife, Melissa, shouts as I hoot out the window. "What happened to...*slow?*"

I reluctantly pull my head back in. Who doesn't love a bit of speed? Jack accelerates even more, and I revel. My instinctual trepidation over Manhattan — the Gordon Gecko greed, the paucity of green, the incisor-like skyscrapers — is swallowed up in the roller-coaster rush of arrival as we fly over the

[handwritten in margin: incisor-like skyscrapers]

water. The multitasking crack of 24/7 connectedness gives me a similar rush. I'm the first to admit that twenty-first-century life triggers pleasant chemistry.

Suddenly, the Williamsburg slam-dunks us into Lower East Side gridlock. Jack slams on the brakes. "Jesus H. Christ on a popsicle stick," he mutters, taking a drag on his cigarette. Garbage bags are piled high on pedestrian-choked Canal Street sidewalks. Taxi exhaust blends with the tobacco smoke. My buzz dies as anxiety balls in my stomach.

I'm an outer-borough boy. My Irish grandparents landed at Ellis Island and raised my father and his two siblings in Queens. I grew up on Long Island. Hence, I've got a bit of *Saturday Night Fever* angst around moving to a Greenwich Village apartment, breaking caste and moving-on-up from a working-class Queens row house. I don't belong in Manhattan.

Melissa, my wife of less than half a year, is scrunched next to me in the van, her hair still wisping around her gorgeous green eyes from the blustery crossing. She cradles a lamp under each arm. Our motivations are essentially at cross-purposes: she is starting a new job as a program specialist at the United Nations that will probably mean working more, while I desire to do less. Will our attempt at Slow City living stretch the bonds of our marriage?

Here is our plan for the year: We'll live a minimalist, leisure-rich, spiritually mindful 12 x 12 life in the world's fastest city. First, we've already shed clutter by downsizing our square footage, moving to a micro-apartment that's 80 percent smaller than our former Queens home. Second, my goal is to work a maximum of only two days a week, freeing up time to interact with the city's cultural creatives who are innovating various facets of Slow. My "five-day weekends" will also allow me time for a whole lot of absolutely nothing. For a work junkie like myself, I figure "simply being" — resisting the urge to *do* for several hours a day in order to seek equanimity — will deeply challenge me. But I reached rock bottom in Queens; I have to slow down, even if Manhattan won't. Third, despite Melissa's full-time job, we've committed ourselves to spending a lot of time on the banks of the Hudson River and in Central Park, to a regular yoga practice, and to fostering daily mindfulness of the beauty of New York, thereby finding balance and joy.

Sounds good, right? But it seems particularly ironic, even perhaps quixotic, as we sit in...traffic. Why seek slow? Slow is an interminable line at the Department of Motor Vehicles. Slow is an old-fashioned rotary phone, the kind that took so long to dial that, as comedian Louis CK jokes, you kind of hated friends who had 0s and 9s in their numbers. Slow is un-American — it's inefficient, dull, and Luddite. It also feels elitist. Only the rich can afford to go slow in Manhattan.

The traffic loosens, and we pick up speed along Canal Street, smoothly turning north on Lafayette, eventually achieving what musicians call *tempo gusto*, or the right speed. We find a balance between the breakneck Williamsburg Bridge and the gridlocked Lower East Side.

My spirits rise. Carlo Petrini, the Italian founder of Slow Food, says, "If you are always slow, then you are stupid. That's not what we're aiming for. Being Slow means that you control the rhythms of your own life. You decide how fast you have to go in any given context.... What we are fighting for is the right to determine our own tempos." Slow is not Luddite. It means cultivating positive qualities — being receptive, *definition of slow* (handwritten margin note)

intuitive, patient, reflective, and valuing quality over quantity — instead of the fast qualities so common today: being busy, controlling, impatient, agitated, acquisitive. Slow is about taking the necessary time to create a new economy centered on self-paced living.

Speaking of which, Melissa and I have worked hard to make our attempt at Slow in Manhattan financially feasible. My previous year's workaholism, combined with the strong savings ethic my father instilled in me, has generated a nest egg of savings that — along with Melissa's salary, a careful monthly budget, and living in a small apartment — makes our plan seem doable.

Jack pulls up in front of our new home: 11 Cornelia Street, between West 4th and Bleecker. The nineteenth-century building is set pleasantly back from the street behind another apartment building. He helps us carry our boxes through a "horse entrance," the high, narrow archway through which — before the automobile — horses passed, to be fed and watered in the area that now serves as the building's little courtyard.

After stacking our boxes in a small mountain, Jack splits, leaving Melissa and me to finish the job. We stare, flummoxed, at the totality of our belongings in the courtyard. It's only a sliver of what we once possessed in Queens, but it's still a lot, especially to carry up five stories of an elevator-less building. Melissa retrieves the two lamps, I grab a box, and we lug our first load up the grungy-carpeted stairwell. I try to remember what our new place looks like. We barely got to see the apartment before signing a one-year lease. Greenwich Village real estate flips in seconds, and to get this place, we had to pay two-months' security deposit within an hour of the viewing.

We're panting when we reach the top floor. I open the door to apartment 10R and step inside.

I feel, for a moment, like there's been a big misunderstanding. The far end of the apartment is just a few steps away. It's two twelve-foot-by-twelve-foot boxes divided by the slenderest of kitchenettes, with a sidecar of a bathroom attached.

I put the carton I'm holding on the floor. Melissa steps hesitantly in, a lamp under each arm, and attempts to walk into the kitchen. She is unable to squeeze through the slim passageway, and the realization dawns: the lamps — and much of the rest of our gear — won't fit. Unable to suppress a frown, Melissa turns and trudges back down the stairs, lamps in hand.

I listen to her footfalls recede. My eyes study this <u>thimble</u> of an apartment. I have utterly forgotten my excitement on the Williamsburg Bridge: we left our Queens home — where we had lived for three years, a lovely place nearly five times bigger — for *this*?

IN 2008, A YEAR AFTER MY EXPERIENCE in a North Carolina 12 x 12, I took over my grandparents' 1938 two-story brick row house on 83rd Place in Queens. One of the first things I did was to remove the crabgrass lawn in the back, trowel in three hundred pounds of manure, and plant two dozen varieties of vegetables and herbs. My grandparents — Nana and Pop — did a similar thing in that identical spot in the 1940s. They created a "Victory Garden" to support the Allied war effort. What a thrill to unearth shards of Nana's china, along with a beet-red glass marble that I imagined belonged to my father, who used to play beside the Victory Garden. What a thrill, too, in Asphalt USA, to daily touch dirt and watch earth fuse with

[handwritten in margin: thimble of an apartment]

seeds, rainstorms, and sun to manufacture butternut squash, whose vines overtook the driveway, and snap peas, which ascended the back-awning poles.

Inside the house, I ripped up Nana and Pop's half-century-worn, musty wall-to-wall carpeting from the living room, dining room, and bedrooms, my sweaty body powdered with mustard yellow dust, the pulverized remains of foam padding. I sliced the carpet into strips, swept, and scrubbed the oak floors until they shined a warm beige.

The next two years brought the typical old-house projects, many of which I attacked myself. Little YouTube videos taught me to caulk and grout, skim coat and apply mildew-resistant bathroom paints. Gradually, the house transformed: The roof was refurbished, the dying boiler replaced, the basement bathroom sheet-rocked, the exterior bricks repointed, the sagging front stoop brought erect. Repairing an old home and learning urban agriculture buoyed my spirits; this "re-skilling" connected me with the sorts of things our grandparents knew but our parents forgot.

During this time, Melissa and I met through a mutual friend from Cochabamba, Bolivia, where she'd been living just before we'd met. As we began to fall in love, Melissa ventured into Queens — a borough she knew nothing of beyond the Nogochi art gallery in Long Island City and good Indian food in Jackson Heights — and soon she started spending the occasional night. Next, her designated drawer in my dresser grew to a whole closet, which grew to moving in. Inspired by upstate farmer Shannon Hayes's book *Radical Homemakers*, we transformed our household from a unit of consumption into a unit of production, reuse, and repair. The Victory Garden bloomed more prolifically than ever, and Melissa and I did morning yoga in the driveway, navigating pumpkin vines during sun salutations. During the warm months, we fed ourselves largely out of our garden, while also drying, freezing, and cellaring food for the winter.

For fruit, we gleaned pears from a long-forgotten pear tree atop the 83rd Place hill. The gnarled hardwood stood defiantly in a small rectangle of weed-choked earth right above the eight lanes of the Long Island Expressway (known to New Yorkers as the LIE). That ancient tree, I surmised, survived Robert Moses, who, in Urban Renewal gusto, sliced the LIE through my grandparents' neighborhood in the 1950s. As Melissa and I picked basketfuls of pears, we could see the jaws of the Manhattan skyline flickering in the distance. The ambition and greed in that nest of power made my insides clench. Sure, I rode the subway into the city every few days to have lunch with Melissa or take in a museum, but I preferred keeping Manhattan at a distance. Leaving the skyline behind, we carried our pears home to a dining-room production line, making fruit salads and tarts and slicing up and freezing the rest for winter.

April brought the pungent scent of wild onion greens, sizzling in the pan with eggs. As I walked home from the subway, I'd harvest the onion greens from sidewalk cracks and people's lawns, shoving fistfuls into my pockets, along with dandelion greens for our salad. Fall brought the ritual abandonment of pumpkins onto the garbage curb, and I'd snatch up the ones not carved into jack-o'-lanterns. Melissa and I sliced the pumpkins for pies to gift to neighbors and blended them into pumpkin puree to freeze, the seeds salted and toasted for snacks.

Our urban archaeology stretched beyond gleaned pears

gleaning food & items put curb-side

and curbed pumpkins to free shopping on Tuesdays, when the city Sanitation Department picks up large items left on the curb. Last year's toaster oven? Found it. Computer chair? Got it. Blender? Naturally. Melissa and I furnished and equipped our home through free shopping, thereby consuming almost nothing new — but consuming nonetheless, as our home filled with possessions we had to clean and maintain. To evade costly home décor updates, we decorated — as blogger Tom Hodgkinson encourages in *The Idler* — in the style of previous eras immune to change. Hodgkinson selected his favorite era, the 1950s, and decorated through thrift shops. We were more eclectic, layering our neighbors' abandonments into Nana and Pop's 1940s furniture, linoleum counters, and chandeliers, along with Melissa's grandfather's landscape paintings.

One evening, the sunset blushing peach through our kitchen window, I wrapped my arms around Melissa's waist as we both looked down over our Victory Garden and the back alley's single large tree, an oak in a neighbor's back patch. The sunset aplay in its leaves, the tree shrouded the alley in a previous-era glow of community, the era of Nana and Pop, when less was usually more, and a slower pace was the norm. I asked Melissa what she was thinking. She didn't reply. I continued to hold her, gazing out at our "pet" squirrel, Mono, as she raced down from her nest along what we loverly-dubbed the SIE (Squirrel Island Expressway): this well-worn path stretched from Mono's nest-branch, down the trunk, and along neighboring fence-tops, before exiting into the Victory Garden. Mono grabbed a cherry tomato and munched. I used to throw one of Nana's silver spoons at Mono, and I even went so far as to spread fox urine along the garden's edges, but I eventually realized Mono's sharecropping percentage was our fee for the pleasure of a wild animal in our lives. The sun was angling harder when Melissa finally spoke. "I was thinking," she said, "about what it would be like to be a Queens mama."

Mama. Implications of not only marriage but children. I suddenly pictured my Nana standing at the same window, opening it to scold, in her Irish brogue, Mono's forebears as they snatched from her Victory Garden while my Dad shot marbles in the driveway, a beet-red one bouncing astray into the thick strawberry patch. Melissa and I hadn't spoken much about marriage, but the question was right beneath the leaves. Our love had grown with the new-old dream we'd woven into the row house and its Victory Garden, into the extraordinary low-carbon subway and bus network that permitted carlessness, into the judiciously used broadband connection that allowed us to engage a fast culture while not becoming absorbed by commuting.

Could this be our life? This hope seduced me even as I knew that, in some ways, the dream was already eroding.

It began at Hot Bagels.

At a certain point in our Queens life we became regulars at Hot Bagels on Eliot Avenue, bringing reusable bags for our fresh bagels. "Two everythings, right in here," I said one morning, opening a canvas bag.

"Wait a minute!" the guy behind the counter replied. "Somebody sent you." He grinned and wagged a large finger at me.

"Actually..." I shrugged. "Nope."

"Somebody else does that. A lady."

"Does what?"

[handwritten margin note: Hot Bagels erodes the dream]

"*That!*" He fingered the canvas bag. Melissa had been picking up the bagels for the past week. And she'd brought...*that.*

Two weeks later, a twenty-something, gum-chewing woman behind the Hot Bagels counter, her soft brown hair in a ponytail, winked at me whilst popping my two everythings in the canvas and said: "Ya girlfriend...she took a bayeg."

Bayeg. I translated from the Queensian: bag.

"You know what else?" she said.

I shifted feet, looked at her name tag: Dawn. Several other employees looked on through half-smirks. They were in on it. "What?"

"I ratted you out, too!" Dawn beamed.

Leaving the shop, I realized that, yes, I'd forgotten my reusable on another day, and Hot Bagels' Stasi double-agent Dawn snitched to Melissa. Humorous, sure, but how bizarre that reusable bags were novel enough to qualify as an inside joke?

The third Hot Bagels incident came several days later on a particularly bad airplane day. For about a year leading up to this, the already noisy LaGuardia Airport flight path over our neighborhood had worsened. The FAA's "NextGen" system used GPS to fly twice as many planes into LaGuardia by spacing them sixty seconds apart. Following Nana's example — my grandmother was a leader in our local civic association — I'd spent the year writing articles in the *Juniper Berry* community magazine about the flight path and starting a small, active Clean and Quiet Skies Coalition. Unfortunately, the vast majority of our Queens neighbors shrugged off our petitions with you-can't-fight-the-FAA apathy. They didn't flinch at studies linking airplane fumes to asthma and airplane noise to long-term, severe stress. Some neighbor kids actually made a game out of plane-spotting — *Delta! American! Jet Blue!* they'd cry as the corporate logos passed just over their heads.

On this particular morning, I'd been unable to concentrate on work — my noise-canceling headphones being useless against the 747s as they rattled our windows — and I'd gone out for a jog, not so much to run, but to run away from the flight path. Before leaving, I'd stuffed a plastic grocery bag in my back pocket. Sweaty after the jog, I entered Hot Bagels and pulled out my two bucks. "Just pop in those everythings, please," I said to Dawn, as I held out my crinkled bag.

Dawn was not smiling. She shook her head vigorously. "No way. That's *weird*."

I'd been up since sunrise with the planes. I was hungry and just wanted bagels. "You've outed me, Dawn," I said, forcing a smile and opening the bag wider.

But Dawn refused. "Too weird." She bit her lip.

Indignity welled up like bile. What's weird, I wanted to announce, is ten million New Yorkers throwing ten million plastic bags into incinerators each day. Weird is the fossil fuels burned to make the plastic bags and ship them here. Weird isn't curbside scavenging, it's clogging the landfills with perfectly usable items. But I didn't say any of this. Instead, I said, simply: "There's too much garbage."

"Yeah, you can say that again," a woman in line snickered, setting off most of the dozen customers behind me in laughter. A guy in a Giants cap shook his head in first-psycho-of-the-day resignation.

Dawn, playing to an audience now, continued: "It's like, what if I were to ask you to put a bagel in this *rubber glove?*" she said, miming the action. "I mean, I might be able to push it into the glove — right? — but it'd be weird."

I glanced at the sad, sweaty plastic bag in my hand. Dawn was correct. I was weird.

"Will you move your ass, buddy?" said a thick-necked guy in a shirt and tie. "Just take the friggin' bag."

I took the friggin' bag.

Feeling, as the locals say, like a total douchebag, I left with head lowered, further rebuked by the sonic boom of an airplane. I recalled something one of my *realpolitik* grad school professors once said to me, cynically, or so I thought at the time: "Bill, I know you're an idealist, and I admire that. But remember this one rock-solid law of life: You don't change an institution or a culture. The institution, the culture...they change you."

Melissa and I had created a Queens culture with precisely two members. That culture had an ideology (*Radical Homemaking*), practices (urban permaculture, re-skilling), and a history (the Golden Age of Nana and Pop). We'd ignited a bottle rocket that blazed its tiny bright trail skyward, but would it only fizzle out as it plunged?

After our "Queens mama" reverie, Melissa and I grew more serious about planning our life together, even as Queens itself became less appealing. She worked at the United Nations as a consultant — not in one of the widely coveted "permanent" positions that are essentially tenured — using the grassroots development skills she'd honed in Bolivia in a UN program to increase women's political participation globally. But her hours grew longer, she telecommuted less, and she returned after dinner many nights, exhausted. As a result, I found it harder, without her companionship and help, to push myself to organize civic association meetings, tend beans, and do yoga amid pumpkin vines. Instead, increasingly over the next year, I did what everyone else did. I worked more.

I wrote more articles for the *Washington Post* and *Atlantic*, sometimes tapping at the keyboard until 2 AM, plagued by airplane-insomnia. I responded to emails at all hours on the smartphone in order to stay in a loop that never seemed to close. I contributed to the flight path above our house by flying off to give lectures and perform consultancies. As a writer, speaker, and international development specialist, I enjoyed the flow of checks arriving in the mail that increased our savings, but I felt increasingly hollow even as my external "success" increased.

Melissa and I were getting caught up in the prevailing turbo-capitalist ethos. In fact, the rush to work was the real reason for the impatience in the morning line at Hot Bagel. Americans work longer hours than the citizens of any other country — fourteen more hours per week than an average European — and on average we leave unused, and so waste, 30 percent of our vacation time. I'd taken on so many work commitments, mostly subconsciously, to fit in and feel valued within this system. I overworked, eating quick meals at the laptop or between flight connections. Even as Melissa and I married, in a small ceremony with family and close friends, our overworking led us to join the disquieting "uni-moon" trend. Instead of a honeymoon trip together in the busy weeks after our wedding, we each took separate, individual vacations without each other — uni-moons, or what amounted to a few days of free time at the end of separate work trips. She took hers in the Dominican Republic after a UN capacity-building workshop; I took mine in Paris on a forty-eight-hour stopover after a community forestry consultancy in Liberia, West Africa.

Strolling, alone, in Montmartre that first evening, I found myself on the smartphone, checking work emails. Looking up from my phone, I was jolted aware that the Eiffel Tower and all of Paris were stretched out before me in all their beauty. I thought back to my North Carolina 12 x 12 and wondered what had happened to one of the big lessons I learned there: the need to balance my constant *doing* with the joy of simply *being* — a kind of Leisure Ethic. I dialed Melissa, but she couldn't talk. "Heading into a meeting, babe," she said.

When I returned to Queens, we began to dream of getting out. Before we met, we'd each worked for several years in Bolivia, and we enjoyed the relaxed and little-commercialized culture there. Also, my beautiful daughter, Amaya, lives in Bolivia. Amaya's mom is Bolivian, and it's difficult for me not to live near my daughter, who at the time was seven years old, even though I support her financially and pay regular visits. Perhaps, Melissa and I both agreed, it was time to admit defeat and leave New York. We couldn't live our ideals here.

Then, two months after our wedding and uni-moons, Melissa was offered a killer promotion.

She'd make more money in this permanent position, sit in a nice private office, and help even more women around the globe. I wanted to support Melissa, but I needed out of New York. "Maybe it's *Queens*," Melissa suggested. "What if we moved into Manhattan?"

She talked about Slow Foodies, LEED architects, and Occupiers. About inspiring spiritual masters and musicians. "Your professor's dictum," she said, "about the culture changing you.... It doesn't apply in Manhattan because that's where they shape the trends that others follow."

That sounded nice, but the thought of advancing suicidally *toward* the beast only made me depressed. Increasingly, I found myself visiting my grandparents' joint grave at St. John's

Cemetery, a ten-block walk from the house. It was one of the few peaceful green spaces around. I'd place a small rock atop their headstone and touch the intricate Celtic cross engraved above their names. Then I'd eat a silent lunch under the big oak above their grave, a tree literally containing something of them.

One day, while I was removing squash beetle pests by hand in the Victory Garden, a truck pulled up and some workers began digging up a neighbor's crabgrass lawn. *Eureka!* I thought, maybe the Victory Garden idea was spreading! But that afternoon, under the roar of 747s, a truck arrived and poured asphalt into the dug-out space, creating a Garden of Defeat.

Finally, rumors surfaced about the big tree in our alley. It could fall on our homes, some said. And it was festering with squirrels.

"They're mocking me," a neighbor told Melissa and me. "The friggin' squirrels in *that* tree!"

"I love that tree," Melissa said.

"Think of the shade it gives on hot summer days," I tried, watching Mono — our happy pet — cruising the SIE.

"They chatter and hiss at me when I come out to my car," he said.

Melissa spotted the tree-removal truck while I was still in bed. She ran out and argued with the home's owner but came back crying. I went out and gave the owner our best arguments. Surprisingly, she agreed with me. "I love that tree, too. But the neighbors are relentless."

"It's your property," I said. "This is on you."

She looked up into the branches, over at the men with chainsaws, and then back at me. I could see she *did* love the tree. She said: "I can live with that."

This wasn't sarcasm. It was resignation. *I can live with that.* I can live with airplanes and asthma. I can live without trees and animals. I can live to work.

I can't live with that.

I walked away. And then I ran.

I ran to the only place with a lot of trees: the cemetery. There, I felt a strange urge to climb the tree above Nana and Pop's grave, so I struggled my way up into the branches. Perched on a high limb, I frowned out at the sharp tips of Manhattan's distant skyscrapers. They pierced the foliage, wanting blood.

Time passed. I heard a voice from below: "Hey."

I looked down. Melissa.

"Hey," I echoed.

"Why don't you come back down?"

I thought, *Come back down to what?*

"Come up," I said.

She squinted at me, arms akimbo. Seeing the intelligent gleam in her eyes, I felt absurd. I was being oversensitive and acting badly, asking her to climb to me. I remembered something a friend said to me from a Lakota Indian elder: "Sometimes I go about pitying myself, when all the time I am carried on great wings across the sky."

Melissa climbed up.

She'd learned mountaineering in the Bolivian Andes. Hold to hold, in no time she was sitting adjacent to me, two primates, unspeaking, on a thick bough.

We sat in the tree for a long time. We touched hands, touched bark. The tree, rooted into Nana and Pop, held us. The top of Manhattan glinted through the leaves. Melissa broke the silence. "Bill, I know you love your grandparents. But you can't

no returning to the slow past - look for a slow future

go back to a slow past. Maybe, together, we can look for a slow future."

Our eyes locked, almost genetically, like fertilization. Then she unlocked and gazed out toward the skyscraper tips, leading my glance, and in this wordless way I knew what she was saying: You build strength not through taking the easy path, but by facing what you most fear. Instead of shuddering at those jaws from a distance, I needed to inhabit the mouth.

We climbed down the tree to the foot of my grandparents' grave. I placed a stone and said good-bye, knowing that it was for good this time. I'd return, but not as a kid on the block. I needed to support Melissa's dream. And I needed to resist the temptation to run away to the equivalent of a 12 x 12 in the forest. Instead, with my wife, I would struggle to somehow create *our* 12 x 12 in the most difficult place on the planet — the hot core of global capitalism, Manhattan.

2. | THE JAM

AT FIRST, MELISSA AND I call it our little ballet: the way we *pas de poisson* past each other and the piles of half-unpacked stuff in our minuscule apartment. But — three days in, novelty out — it's clearly punk slam dancing in an undersized mosh pit. We bang shoulders, bruise shins on bed edges, and curse over the four-inch-by-eight-inch kitchen counter.

"Is Bloomberg high?" Melissa lashes out one evening after slicing her finger while dicing a carrot on a cutting board straddling sink and stove. "I'm already sick of his micro-apartment initiative!"

I'm in the East Wing — our living/dining/*only* room — baffled by the byzantine directions for the Ikea fold-up table we purchased specifically to fit this space. Scrotally colliding with the edge of our tiny fireplace, I wedge into the kitchenette with Melissa and kiss her finger. It's bleeding, but just barely. I grope for a bright side. "We need just three lights in our entire pad," I

need only 3 lights to illuminate whole 'pad'

announce. "And look at that one tiny heater! Our carbon foot-print is a fifth of what we had in Queens."

"But my carbon *foot* is five times bigger than this apartment," she says, soaping up her finger. "This feels like carbon foot-binding."

I know. To bathe in our fish-tank bathtub — it's three feet long — I adapt the yoga pose "shoulder stand": Head in the water, flush against the tub. Butt against the other end. Feet at a ninety-degree angle up the wall.

Then there's the toilet. It's impossible to shut the bathroom door when you sit because — I measured it — there's just 10¾ inches between the front edge of the toilet seat and the door. I imagine an awkward moment of having to leave the apartment when a guest asks to use the restroom so that they might answer nature's call with the door ajar.

And that same bathroom door only opens outward eleven inches before meeting the bedroom's queen-sized bed.

It's one thing, I discover, to live 12 x 12 in serene solitude, the gurgle of No Name Creek ribboning through your perma-culture orchards. It's quite another for a twosome to squeeze into a double-wide 12 x 12 in an impure polis.

Sure, we've winnowed our belongings way down from Queens. But we still have far too much. Moving boxes flaunt their bulk; four large paintings stand at accusatorily stiff attention against the fireplace. Where to put it all? New York City Mayor Michael Bloomberg's micro-apartment initiative embraces architectural minimalism, allowing for apartments smaller than the four-hundred-square-foot minimum required by the city's zoning laws. The logic makes sense: let folks pay cheaper rents and burn less fossil fuels. But 340 square feet just ain't right.

Besides, minimalism is just another excuse to buy. A billion-dollar annual retail industry has sprung up to sell us all the things we need to live with less. Besides the magical Ikea folding dining room table, there's a cornucopia of niche items still too new to be discarded for easy curbside plucking. Melissa comes home from work one day with shopping bags full of razor-thin hangers to wedge 13 percent more clothes into our single closet, clever fabric drawers to resuscitate the dead space under our bed, and magnetic spice jars that allow the suspension of thyme from the edge of a Frigidaire.

At first, we toss these bags of space savers onto our despotic, still-unpacked crap pile, when a better solution appears. An index card is taped above our mailboxes at the bottom of the stairwell: "Moving Sale," it reads. "Everything must go. Call or stop by 6B." At the bottom it's signed: "Wanda and Dave."

Apartment 6B is our exact 340-square-foot floor plan, two stories down! Enthused, Melissa and I knock on Wanda and Dave's door that evening. We'll score space-savers at a bargain, we reason, and see how another couple has elegantly navigated minimalism's rough waters.

The door opens, and Wanda, a slim woman in her late twenties, invites us inside.

The ensuing encounter is surreal. Though identical to ours, Wanda's apartment feels a fraction of the size. Entering, I feel the same sense of constrained claustrophobia as under the low-ceilinged Floor 7½ in the film *Being John Malkovich*, but it's not from the ceiling. Wanda and Dave have entombed the contents of a macro-apartment inside of a micro.

"This is Dave's recording studio," Wanda says with a curt, ironic laugh. A profusion of audio mixers and tower speakers muscle their way around a full-sized sofa. Their flat-screen television overwhelms one wall. Unable to move corporeally, I swivel my head and squint into the dim kitchen swollen with food processors, salad spinners, and all manner of pots and pans. I can hardly breathe. My heart ticks faster. The walls close in like the trash-compactor scene in *Star Wars*. Wanda says: "I probably shouldn't point this out since you guys are just moving in. But living in 340 square feet..." She pauses, twisting up her face. "It's not *human*."

We leave Wanda and Dave's micro-hoarding initiative, unhelped and uncomforted. Outside the building is no better. Sweaty garbage bags bunker around the Papaya Dog fast-food joint ("99 Cent French Fries!"), which leak a permanent puddle that willfully stinks up the triangle where Cornelia meets Sixth Avenue. A half dozen porn shops — their windows displaying a confounding blend of S&M whips and whimsical "fundies" (underpants for two) — line the square block around us on Sixth Avenue and 4th Street. Interspersed among the porn stores are tattoo parlors with plate-glass windows, through which leathery men with ink guns can be seen carving devil's crosses into teenage torsos. Meanwhile, the Cornelia Street crack dealer stalks new clients.

"*Our* crack dealer," an apartment neighbor puts it to me — he skirts nocturnally no matter the hour. Skinny, beak-nosed, mustached, with a Mediterranean complexion, he eyes me one evening and approaches as I return from the Korean grocer.

Ah, but for Queens! Its harmless little flight path and Hot Bagels slights! They hack down trees and vanquish squirrels, but at least there's sky above the two-story row houses. Here, apartment towers carve up the heavens, and there's nary a cemetery respite from the asphalt.

"Partying tonight?" the dealer asks, sporting a zombie-like "I'm-here-for-the-gang-bang" grin. I shake my head and flee through our horse entrance, up the dim stairwell, and into our overstuffed micro. I'm boxed in, no exit. Melissa's working late. I'm lonely, hyperstimulated, and far from the balm of nature. I've changed locations but not demons.

THE NEXT DAY, still a little shell-shocked by my glancing encounter with the crack dealer, I venture across Sixth Avenue and wander into Washington Square Park. Its eight acres burst with daffodils and tulips, bird- and human-song.

In fact, the park is a barrage of music that at first feels almost as overstimulating as the city itself. To the north, a New York University female a cappella group harmonizes through white-toothed smiles. To the west, a large black man plays two trumpets at once — one horn at each corner of his mouth, like tusks — then repeatedly bellows "Do-NAAY-tions!" and passes a hat. To the east, a short, wiry man wheels a grand piano into the walkway, cracks his knuckles, and cajoles out Chopin and Mozart. To the south, an on-tour Korean Christian rock band singer cries out, "Does Jesus save?" A passerby shouts, "Hell yeah!"

In the center of all this, near the fountain, I see a thin, thirty-something black man, accompanied by a multiethnic mix of five other musicians, crooning Marvin Gaye's "What's Going On?" I walk over and sit on a concrete bench facing them. *We've got to find a way*, the man belts out, *to bring some lovin' here today!* Yellow and white tulips blow in the breeze, and the tune, which is really about what I need most — healing — eases off, then rebuilds in tempo and pitch. I feel a bit of the urban craziness dissolve, and I'm amazed that only a dozen others have gathered around these geniuses.

I remain transfixed on the bench as the music segues from seventies soul to the Beatles to a little reggae, then to the theme song from the old TV series *The Jeffersons*. "Movin' On Up" is sung with smiles and laughter. The crowd builds to a few dozen. I find myself sometimes clapping along, other times singing, always tapping my toe. The musicians — two Latino, two black, and two white, who play a mix of guitars, bass, conga drums, and harmonica — take turns leading songs, but one of them is obviously at the inspirational center, the body of a starfish with five radiating arms.

With a plump belly hanging over his jeans, unpretentious wire-rimmed glasses, and a balding crown, Bruce's rather ordinary, middle-aged appearance belies the vigorousness of his guitar plucking and strumming, the range of his voice, and the acuity of his blue eyes. As the music crescendos, I notice tears in the eyes of the woman sitting next to me on the bench. There's a mounting cohesion between crowd and musician. The Temptations song seems almost to sway with the Empire State Building rising to the north of the Washington Square Arch. Building, arch, and music lilt and flow like something Gaudi or Picasso might paint, and people clap and hoot for more.

Several days pass. Each afternoon I jump the Papaya Dog puddle, cross Sixth Avenue, and join Bruce and his ever-changing configuration of musicians and hangers-on in Washington Square Park. It's got a name, I discover: it's known as the Jam.

"Bruce started the Jam seven years back," one of the musicians, a drummer, tells me as we chat between songs. "It's his gift to the city."

"But he always seems to be here," I say. "How does he earn a living?"

"Dude works 24/7!"

I'm perplexed. I've only once seen a tip jar out. The Jam seems unconcerned with the monetary economy.

The drummer smiles. "Twenty-four hours a *week*, brother. Seven months a *year*."

The air of leisure hovering around the Jam intrigues me. I ask the Jam's regular dancer — Monica — about this. She's a slim-figured, late-thirties woman with curly chestnut hair. "Like Bruce and a lot of the others who hang with us," she tells me between songs, "I work to live, not the reverse." A writer, Monica says she works on her laptop under the trees in the park or, on cold or rainy days, in favorite cafés and library nooks.

"But how do you afford New York?" I ask.

She takes a plastic container out of her backpack. "See this wheat-berry salad? Last night's dinner. And it's my lunch and dinner today. Along with some apples. And there's something like five hundred free things to do in New York every day, including the Jam. Plus...I live in a broom closet!"

Living in a virtual closet myself, I don't romanticize Monica's even tinier quarters. Still, as I chat with her and other Jammers, a theme surfaces: they work for *time* as much as for money, and they earn that time by living smaller, simpler, and smarter. Bruce, for example, is a self-employed computer programmer who works as much as required and not an hour more. These Jammers have what author and activist Vicki Robin calls a "joy-to-stuff ratio" of a very different sort from our neighbors back in Queens.

Granted, some of the notions tossed around the Jam are anarchic and bizarre. Between tunes one afternoon, someone gripes about high unemployment, and a guy tuning his mandolin says: "Screw full employment. We should aim for the

joy to stuff ratio

opposite." Oscar Wilde said much the same in his 1891 *The Heart of Man under Socialism*: "It is to be regretted that a portion of the community should be practically in slavery, but to propose to solve the problem by enslaving the entire community is childish." An irresponsible sentiment, Wilde's — and deliciously so — but certainly more honest and witty than the more prevalent notion articulated by his contemporary, the essayist Thomas Carlyle: "Man was created to work, not to speculate, or feel, or dream," Carlyle wrote, adding, "Every idle moment is treason."

The Jam invites me to muse, treasonously — as I decide to start my two-day workweek after a few weeks of vacation to kick off the Slow Year — on whether the idea of a "job" is unfit for the twenty-first century. Why do citizens of America, the world's richest country, work the longest hours and take the shortest vacations? Aren't the time-saving machines and processes we've ingeniously created supposed to...save time?

In his book *How to Be Idle*, British author Tom Hodgkinson — drawing from the work of historian E. P. Thompson — points out that the creation of the job is a relatively recent phenomenon, born out of the Industrial Revolution. Before the eighteenth-century's steam-powered engines and factories, work was a more improvisational affair. People worked, sure, and they did "jobs," but the idea of being yoked to a particular employer at the exclusion of other money-making activities was unusual. For my own part, during a decade living in Africa and South America, I have puzzled over how subsistence agriculturists live mostly outside of the modern economy, and quite happily, scheduling their work by the seasons and by their moods. A Bolivian farmer, for instance, might chop wood one day, then pick kiwis the next, and then take the next three days mostly off to idle over chess or soccer with friends, the joy-to-stuff ratio of his adobe hut making even your average Jammer look opulent. These are self-paced, not employer-paced, lives.

The following day, I watch Monica smiling over her laptop under a tree, listen to Bruce riff wildly, and wonder how they've managed to stay largely self-paced in a society where our very self-esteem is cinched to our work. *Man was created to work, not to speculate, or feel, or dream.* Myself and most self-employed people I know usually become our own exacting bosses, over-scheduling ourselves — as I did in Queens — and not just to keep up with the bills. Working hard is a status symbol and even a patriotic obligation. However, is this just a myth conveniently created by the rich who, as social critic Bertrand Russell notes, "preach the dignity of labor, while taking care themselves to remain undignified in this respect"?

I crack open, for the first time, a new pocket-sized, leather-bound notebook that a friend from La Paz gave me the last time I visited Bolivia. There's a saying in that country: *Caminar preguntando.* "Walk questioning." As part of the Slow Year experiment, I've decided to carry the notebook with me, writing down questions and thoughts that bubble to the surface. Bruce's strumming something mellow. Half-listening, I write a question on the notebook's first page. For a deeply conditioned worker bee like myself, it releases a mix of conflicting feelings.

Is idleness treason?

AFTER A FEW DAYS WITH THE JAM, I see the dilemma of our micro-apartment in a new light. Maybe 340 square feet is not, as per Wanda downstairs, "inhuman." Philosopher Thomas

Freedom bcs he was out of the main house

Merton called his stark monk's chambers "the four walls of my new freedom." How can I approach our micro-apartment in this same spirit? Shouldn't lower rent and less stuff mean more free time?

One day while Melissa is at work, I stream Marvin Gaye on Grooveshark and tackle the problem of our stuff. I tinker with the micro-pad puzzle. Stashing Melissa's unopened space savers in the hallway — intending to return most of them to the store — I unpack our boxes and create two piles: keepers and throwbacks. The latter, far larger pile is to be gifted, thrift-shopped, or stored in a small corner of the building's basement, which our superintendent has agreed to let us use. To accommodate the keepers, I install shelving and hooks, which I have already acquired from a different vacated apartment nearby, whose exiting tenants were happy for me to scavenge their leavings.

In the evening, Melissa and I make further refinements. We stow a minimal kit of kitchenware, toiletries, clothing, and books as if equipping a houseboat's trim hull. It's a refreshing purge; the apartment seems to expand with each tweak. Yet one meddlesome detail remains: the stack of large paintings glaring at us from where they lean against the fireplace.

We've been avoiding the issue. They were painted by her late grandfather, Alexander Crane — Fafa to his grandkids — a professional artist. We both love them.

"There's wall space," Melissa says doubtfully.

We've already shed most of the twenty wall hangings we had in Queens. Now it's the Final Four. But having tested available wall space in the micro, we've agreed that only one can be hung without creating a sense of clutter.

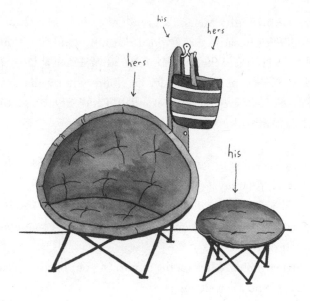

"They're my babies," she says, walking over to gingerly touch a canvas.

The Minimalism Czar in me steels himself. "Which of your babies," I say, doing my best Schwarzenegger, "do you love the most?"

Melissa winces. "Ouch."

"Think of Wanda and Dave," I plead. "Let's try?"

We do. She breathes deep and selects her favorite — the rest to be shipped to her relatives.

Over the next weeks below deck, Melissa and I both feel our well-being rise in proportion to what's been shed. A chaotic apartment begins to transform. A slim metal table in the kitchen welcomes the cutting board; jackets laze on his-and-her hooks; sandals snuggle in their micro-shoe-apartment beside the door. We improvise a kitchen two-step, a bathroom waltz.

Most surprisingly, Melissa's grandfather is closer to us than ever. That's because the stripped-down tranquility of our Zen perch counteracts the overstimulation of Papaya Dog, porn, and our crack-pusher outside, its cloud-white walls drawing the eyes to a beauty mark: Alexander "Fafa" Crane's gold-and-fuchsia watercolor of cliffs and snow.

AFTER SOME WEEKS AS A SPECTATOR, I'm approached by the Jam. "You play?" Bruce asks.

I clear my throat. "Childhood piano lessons," I say. "And high school band trombone.... But I love to just sing and clap along if that's okay."

Bruce fingers a lick on the guitar. "As our brother pleases," he says. "You are welcome."

They play. After a couple songs, Melissa arrives in a lilac suit dress, laptop bag over her shoulder. I rush to hug her. We sit on a bench to listen to the same skinny African American guy who sang Marvin Gaye's "What's Going On?" my first day in the park. Now he's finishing the Temptations' "Papa Was a Rolling Stone," and Bruce's face looks ecstatic as he cries out, "Take it through the roof!" Things build even more. "*Break* through the roof!" The small crowd goes nuts.

Songs. More of them. The side of Melissa's body warms mine. The sun slips behind buildings stacked to the west, painting the Washington Square Arch crimson. A guy in dress slacks and opal cuff links, whom I've never seen play with the Jam before, strums his guitar and sings Otis Redding's "Sitting on the Dock of the Bay," which flows languidly, carrying Melissa and me with it as we hold hands and watch the crimson peel off the arch. Melissa says: "This sensation reminds me of childhood, in Santa Fe, when the parched arroyo near our house would gush with rainwater on monsoon-season afternoons. Do you know, when the rain stopped, we'd head down to the arroyo and just watch it flow?"

Bruce and the other vocalists dip into the cuff-linked guy's lead; Melissa and I sing along, just "wasting time." But are we, Melissa and me? I feel our Queens culture of two expand to a culture of two dozen, as if our micro-apartment's walls are also expanding to include at least this part of the park.

Later, as Melissa and I walk back to Cornelia, light streams from headlights, shop fronts, and apartment windows. We talk about how perplexing it is to square a treasonous timelessness with a scheduled city life — particularly hers at this point. And then we're through the Cornelia Street horse entrance and up the five flights to our stark-white abode. Melissa lights a candle in each window.

The next morning is bright and blue, and Melissa has an idea. "Let's break through the roof," she says, pointing at the ceiling.

I hesitate, thinking that Bruce didn't mean that *literally*, but Melissa isn't asking for my opinion. She's already flying out the door and taking the steps two at a time to the forbidden door to the roof. The leasing agent told us it's "heavily alarmed" and "totally off-limits."

I chase after her.

"I have this suspicion," she says at the top, "that they're just trying to scare us off." She places her hand on the bright red "Alarm Will Sound" handle.

I wince. "Wait!"

She pushes.

With a velvety swoosh, the door sails open and light gushes into the cave-like stairwell. Melissa steps onto the roof. Squinting, I follow.

A hundred buildings rise in discordant geometry and texture. The air smells fresher, summery, a salty breeze coming off the brackish Hudson. The sun threads a gap between two buildings, and I feel it on my face, feel it burning up the walls I've been living in. I've boxed myself in with expectations.

Manhattan will eat me. My mind built that box. *Our apartment's too cramped.* Built that, too. *There's no sky in the city.* My wife just took us through the roof.

Where are all the boxes now?

As Melissa soaks in the sun, I gaze at the Freedom Tower under construction at the Ground Zero site a half mile to the south. "Look!" Melissa cries.

In the sheltered space under the tree canopy that we've seen through our bedroom window, atop a wrought-iron fire escape on an adjoining brick apartment building, sit two adorable puffballs: baby mourning doves, looking almost ready to leap.

3. ROOFTOP BEES AND BEANS

FROM OUR PERCH ON TAR BEACH — our name for our newly discovered, silver-coated tar roof — we watch the baby doves grow. The pair of fluffy dandelion-seed heads bob side by side. The chicks bounce softly between the fire escape of the adjoining building and, for longer stints each day, a thick bough on the tree. When the wind blows, they sway with the tree, sticking to the stretch of branch above the fire escape, presumably to avoid the five-story freefall. Every so often Mom swoops in, usually from the direction of Washington Square Park, and alights beside her babies. Seeing her, they instantly switch from cottony composure to noisy wing-flapping, stabbing their beaks into Mom's mouth for her gourmet regurgitation. After each feeding, she flies off again.

Melissa designates two old seat covers as "beach cushions" to carry up for dove-viewing breakfasts. Each morning we sip coffee and eat baguettes from Amy's Bread, the local bakery where Cornelia meets Bleecker Street a half block from our apartment. Inspired by the time-rich Jam, Melissa uses some of her annual leave to add two days to a three-day weekend, and these five spontaneous days off become not only a Greenwich Village stay-cation but also something of the honeymoon we were too busy to take together in our hectic "uni-moon" days.

But what to do on our stay-cation? Ten thousand Big Apple activities beckon. We narrow them down to three. First, activate one of the Internet Age's crowning achievements: the vacation email auto-response. Second, turn off cell phones and laptops. Third, extract batteries from said contraptions, stashing the batteries far from them. Voila! All stay-cation activities accomplished with five days to go.

Treasonously unscheduled and incommunicado, we idle away day one, a Thursday, leaving the nest a half-dozen times, but only to climb the twelve steps to Tar Beach. The day opens up something of what cultural ecologist David Abram calls "the more than human world." During our rooftop lunch we're mostly silent, watching two flocks of pigeons merge into a single flock, disconnect again, then reconnect, like lava in a lamp, while navigating the surrounding buildings. Suddenly, the flocks separate and begin doing figure-eights. Melissa whispers: "Double helixes!" Later I bring up our French press with coffee, pour it into mugs. The light filters through the muddy pour, through the tree's green canopy. A red-tailed hawk, wings stiff as kites, soars over Tar Beach toward Washington Square Park. As the sun mellows into its evening colors, we realize we have not seen another face of our species the whole day, just the occasional hominoid shape through an adjacent apartment window.

During our five days, we do go out, following unplanned idle whims. We savor the Met's sacred Astor Court, delight in Slow Food at Marienella's on Carmine, and hop the Staten Island Ferry with our old bikes to hit the beach. But the bulk of our activity remains in the tiny triangle between apartment, Tar Beach, and Washington Square Park, where we venture beyond the Jam to a curious chap known as William the Pigeon Guy.

He's a little Don Draper in appearance — handsome, dark-haired, fortyish, always immaculately dressed in chinos, leather shoes, and pressed shirts — and he feeds pigeons organic almonds from his mouth.

Melissa asks William about the pigeons. He obliges with a torrent of information. For starters, there's the pigeon named Chico on his forearm. After Chico's mother was devoured by a red-tailed hawk, William raised the fledgling in a sewing kit in his apartment, feeding him milk from an eyedropper. Chico, now two years old, is distinguished by the beige feathers setting him apart from the others in their blue-and-gray. "Every light-colored pigeon you see around here," William says a little proudly, "is one of Chico's kids."

William is a high-end real estate broker who, between appointments showing clients fancy downtown apartments, chills with the birds. With William, I feel for the first time the surprisingly warm feet of a pigeon. He pours some almonds in my cupped hand, and Chico bounds onto my forearm. Another pigeon swooshes in and lands beside him. They eat, and then simply continue to hang out on me. William gives Melissa some almonds, too, and a bird lands on her. Chico clutches at my arm, seemingly happier with us than with other pigeons.

"They feel safer from the hawks when they're with humans," William explains. "They'll linger for hours."

Melissa tells William about our Tar Beach aviary, and he rattles off facts about "squeaker-phase" baby pigeons and doves. The reason, he tells us, that you never see baby pigeons in parks is because they grow up in secluded roof nests like ours, reaching — quite incredibly — full size in a matter of weeks. "That's a four-week-old right there!" William says, pointing to a Chico-sized pigeon.

As Chico's gizzard mixes and mashes the nuts he's eaten (William: "They've got small rocks, shells, and sand in there to break 'em down, in the absence of teeth"), factoids and even time itself slip away. Chico and I gaze at each other, winged-to-legged, as trumpets resound from the man who plays two horns at once — those tusks! — and a little girl spins a pink hula hoop to the music.

Melissa interrupts my reverie. "In Queens they're making enemies of the wildlife," she says. "Here, people connect with the animals." I nod. William is quiet now, maybe thinking about his next real-estate showing, maybe relaxing, as I am, into the Jam, whose music fills the vacuum left by the tusked trumpeter as he asks for "Do-NAY-tions!" Late-afternoon light lacquers the four old buildings guarding the park's west end, brightens the purple NYU flags on rooftops, and gilds the arch's crown.

Tuesday morning arrives: the final Tar Beach breakfast of our stay-cation. Melissa kisses me and leaves for work. Energized by nondoing, I'm determined to work my butt off — within my two-day limit — to get more. It's as if the Cornelia Street crack dealer teased me with a dose of highly addictive idleness, and now I need to hustle for another fix.

My go-to is Tim Ferriss. His book *The 4-Hour Workweek* — yes, four, though it's a playful title, not a literal one — suggests you use two principles at the same time: 80/20 and the Hodgkinson's Principle. The 80/20 principle says that we accomplish 80 percent of work results in just 20 percent of our time. Conversely, we more or less waste the other 80 percent of our time on a paltry 20 percent of the results. Dutifully, I 80/20 my week and find that the principle holds true. Of all the potential work streams — in international consulting, writing, and speaking — that I could pursue, I distill out this week's most strategic one in terms of income-to-time-invested and my current level of enthusiasm: a high-end magazine article.

Then I overlay the Hodgkinson's Principle. Hodgkinson's says that work expands to fill the amount of time available to accomplish it. Thus, having chosen the one most critical work activity, I corral it into a tight timeframe.

Granted, using these two principles a la Ferriss won't be ideal for everyone or all the time. This approach is more suited to entrepreneurs and hourly workers able to prioritize their own time and tasks, nailing the most important ones as quickly as possible and thus freeing up time. But almost anyone, Ferriss notes, can create a small sideline work stream and apply these principles; eventually, perhaps, this side income might become one's main income. For me, thanks to Ferriss and much java, I condense what might have been five days of work into two. Then it's Thursday again, the cusp of five days off.

That sublime Thursday morning — Melissa and much of the city already hustled off to the office — I continue to linger in bed, reading this gem from nineteenth-century English poet Charles Lamb:

> Who first invented work — and bound the free
> And holy-day rejoicing spirit down
> To the ever-haunting importunity
> Of business, in the green fields, and the town —
> To plough, loom, anvil spade — and oh! Most sad
> To that dry drudgery at the desk's dead wood?

Who, indeed. Still in my PJs, I rise and breakfast with our ever-larger "squeaker-phase" pigeons — they've now ventured along the tree branch well beyond fire-escape safety — then dress and stroll past the magnificent townhouses of Bank Street toward the Hudson's Pier 45, a park jutting into the river. I'm a little giddy; there's 148 hours of time-wealth in my crack pipe. I cross the West Side Highway with its six lanes of taxis, FedEx trucks, and buses; cross the bike path with its smattering of bladers, cyclists, and runners; and finally reach the pier-park. As I walk out along it, the West Side Highway decrescendos and the sound of water lapping on pylons rises. Statue of Liberty in the distance. Seagulls crying overhead. The occasional boat sailing by. I come to the end, plop down, dangle bare feet toward the Hudson, and start humming Otis Redding's "Sitting on the Dock of the Bay."

An hour passes, per the Lackawanna clock tower across the river in Hoboken. Then two. I'm still sitting, wasting time. The rest of the morning's bread, some cheese, and an apple in my satchel, I eat when hungry, at one point singing John Lennon's "Watching the Wheels," a tune rhapsodizing "no longer riding on the merry-go-round," but rather just enjoying the way wheels spin. The song brings to mind Lennon and Yoko Ono and their famous Bed-In where, in 1969, they spent a week doing absolutely nothing for world peace.

In the afternoon, Lady Liberty blushes deeper green as the sun angles west. I stand up occasionally to strike the minimal yoga poses needed to contentedly continue my Pier-In. The Hudson swells as the Atlantic tide pushes back on it, and I pull out a copy of seventeenth-century haiku-poet Bashō's *Journey to the Deep North:*

> Listen! a frog
> Jumping into the stillness
> Of an ancient pond

Watching the river, I savor that. Then:

> A weathered skeleton
> in windy fields of memory,
> piercing like a knife

I don't leave the pier all day. At one point while enjoying Bashō, I realize that this Slow Thursday arises out of an idea

I absorbed from Bruce and the Jam: be countercyclical. If the crowd is going one way, do a 180 and saunter in the other direction. There's abundant space on a pier when nearly everyone else is scurrying about the island.

As the sun sinks into New Jersey, tango dancers gather on the pier. Antique music rises from a boom-box. To the sound of the nineteenth-century bandolon, the dancers stalk their way through tango walks. Swift foot-snaps. Head flicks to promenade. The dancers blend with the hazy sunset, and I'm thrilled to watch the wheel they form spin round and round.

The following day, I return to Pier 45. But it feels different. It's partly overcast, and fog dulls the Statue of Liberty. The Hudson's gray, her tide low. Being countercyclical, it seems, isn't about routine.

So I leave the pier, strolling southward. The breezy Hudson is dotted with sailboats and barges. A vendor sells New York pretzels out of a truck. The West Side Highway stops and starts as the traffic breathes with the lights, which tick in unison from green to yellow to red and back. For a while it's absorbing, the sensory nature of being a flaneur, or a passive gazer into the life of a city, but I'm restless today. I'm making a routine out of routine's absence and thereby habituating to nondoing.

This is hardly the idyllic banks of No Name Creek beside the 12 x 12 in North Carolina. In Battery Park, tourist helicopters buzz — wasp-like, aggressive — along the river. A parade of folks vent their stresses into cell phones. One of them, a painfully thin, jumpsuit-clad woman, tugs along a Labradoodle on its leash and yells into her phone, "I'm visibly shaking!" I catch a snippet of the drama: Her doorman failed to greet her, *again*, and he refused to apologize. "The shmuck should be fucking fired!" she screams, yanking her dog along. "I'm going to the co-op board…"

Across a dazed river, a fire burns in Jersey City, billowing black smoke. Twin speedboats blaze north. *I'm visibly shaking* echoes in my head.

MY SHIRT SWEAT-SOAKED, hands covered with soil, I weed the pea rows of Brooklyn Grange, the world's largest rooftop soil farm. I've been at it for two hours as a volunteer, and I feel marvelous. From this full acre of cropland atop the Standard Oil Building in Long Island City, I can see the glistening spread of Manhattan's buildings just across the East River. But mostly it's a big sky feeling. The farm is higher than anything right around it, so I have little sense of the buses and cars and commerce seven stories below.

It's Saturday, day three of my five-day weekend, and I feel particularly good. As I weed, I realize what John Drake writes about in *Downshifting: How to Work Less and Enjoy Life More*. Drake, an overworked executive, took the leap into early retirement only to find that it's not enough to just eliminate the labor that's causing unhappiness; it's also key to fill the vacuum with activities that nourish you. I gerrymandered my workweek into a two-day shape, but the Jam and Pier 45 aren't enough. Enter rooftop farming.

Carrying a full bucket of weeds to the compost pile, I glance over to the far side of the farm at the silhouette of Anastasia Cole Plakias. She is thirty with thick brown hair, and from a football field away, I watch her petite outline confidently directing another work crew. Anastasia cofounded Brooklyn Grange in 2009, along with Gwen Shantz and Ben Flanner.

*opening words
example ?*

After securing a ten-year lease from Acumen Capital Partners, they went to work: fitting the roof with a thick plastic root-barrier, craning up thousands of soil sacks, and shaping earth into rows studded with tomato seedlings and chard plugs. Slowly, a farm took shape.

Today, the farm, built as a green-roof system, holds 1.2 million pounds of soil — and yes, experts verified that the 1919 building can bear the weight. The farm's soil is a special mix of compost and porous stones, which eases the load, and in it grows a variety of organic produce sold to Manhattan and Brooklyn restaurants. Several seasons in, the Grange not only turns a healthy profit but has just expanded by 150 percent to new roofs in the Brooklyn Navy yards.

As we work, I say to Julie, a Columbia graduate student and fellow volunteer, "This is the twenty-first-century Victory Garden, brought to scale."

Julie nods and enthuses about how farmers' markets and restaurants get ultra-fresh, subway-delivered produce with a zero transport footprint. "This is just a piece of the future green city," she says, "where a single lightweight thirty-story tower of recycled materials could supply produce for a quarter million people through hydroponics on each floor. Skyscraper agriculture."

I suggest we start with what exists now, wondering aloud what would happen if just 2 percent of the city's roughly one million rooftops came under cultivation. Twenty thousand asphalt antidotes, minisanctuaries harboring wildlife, purifying the air, and providing contact with nature.

Then, another volunteer tells me Anastasia logs backbreaking eighty-hour weeks, which reminds me of my own pattern of do-gooding over a decade as an aid and conservation worker abroad. Helpful work, most of it — feeding refugees, starting community-based ecotourism projects, and reporting on injustices in the media — but the insane hours taxed my mental and emotional well-being. I wonder about Anastasia: will her drive to forge the planet's *biggest* (best! world-changing!) rooftop farm, while thrilling, also lead to burnout?

After another hour, I take a break and wander over to the chicken coop, where Anastasia is leading a farm tour for elementary schoolchildren from the South Bronx. "Where's the McNugget?" asks a third-grader in an oversized Yankees cap.

"What do you mean?" Anastasia asks. She's cradling a six-pound rosecomb chicken under her right arm, and the coop behind her brims with all color of fowl. There's an awkward silence. The chicken wiggles in Anastasia's arm. The other kids turn their heads to the kid in the Yankees cap, who struggles to clarify. "I mean," he says, "what part of the chicken…is the McNugget?"

Anastasia explains that one McNugget might contain bits of a thousand different chickens — it's a "McFrankenstein creation," she says, of blended-up industrial poultry, steroid-pumped birds pressed into familiar shapes.

"Gross," a little girl next to me mutters. Anastasia may be petite, but she's no-nonsense. New York City–raised, she has a missionary's enthusiasm for urban farming. As she goes on about the phenolic antitoxin chemical preservatives and anti-foaming agents used in making McNuggets, I squirm, concerned that this is too graphic for these little guys. But I soon see that her candidness is working with these kids. Their gazes lock on Anastasia, and I sense they appreciate the truth.

Then the children come up to touch the chicken Anastasia's holding, and another dimension of Brooklyn Grange opens up to me. It's an environmental education facility where urban kids can connect with basil on the stem and real chickens without having to travel upstate. But later in the tour, by the beehives, Anastasia says the word "environment" one too many times. A girl with her hair tied back in a dozen braids says: "Why you keep talking about the en-*vi*-ro-ment? Got nothing to do with us."

Anastasia shoos away a bee. "Where do you think the environment is?"

The girl sets her hands on her hips and scowls, as if to say: *Why do I have to explain every little stupid thing to teachers?* "It's out there!" she exclaims, thrusting an arm, her finger forming an arrow pointing to...what?

I trace the girl's invisible line. It shoots out of her fingertip and over the farm, traversing subway yards, slate-gray warehouses, and the East River. The line vaults the Empire State Building, Times Square, and the doves of Tar Beach. It crosses Hoboken and the subdivisions and strip malls of New Jersey, finally hitting the place where land and sky meet. The end of her line is the horizon.

With a heavy heart, I leave the tour and go back to harvesting rosemary and weeding arugula. My own "white privilege" — the cozy advantages of race and class — are part of what frees me up for rarified pursuits like pier-sitting, Jamming, and rooftop farming. A bunch of chickens and peas won't bridge the chasm between twentieth-century urbanization and wild nature. Living Slow feels, right now, particularly utopian. I know what the girl means — "the environment" is out there, not in here, in the city — but other layers surface. In Liberia, I once heard the horizon poetically defined like this: Run, run, run toward it; you'll never reach it. The end of the line — *nature* — is the horizon. Run, run, run toward it; we'll never reach it.

4. TAKING BACK YOUR TIME

MY FRIEND JOHN DE GRAAF CHUCKLES as we stand side by side atop Tar Beach one Friday morning. "Humanity — obsessed by growth!" he cries out, and the words echo through the narrow courtyards below.

His chuckle turns into a laugh. De Graaf — a few inches shy of my six feet, with an oval face and wide-rimmed glasses — is executive director and cofounder of Take Back Your Time, a Seattle-based nonprofit that "fights to end time poverty" through public education and advocacy for policies like job-sharing, shorter workweeks, and increased vacation leave. His merry demeanor and knack for storytelling bring to mind a mythical Bolivian figure called Ekeko, the jovial Inca who spent his life traveling around cheering people up.

"What do you mean?" I ask, smiling. De Graaf's enthusiasm is contagious.

edit to use as a reading?

"Have you heard David Brower's sermon, the Six Days of Creation?"

I shake my head. He gazes out toward Wall Street's towers and says: "Brower — who founded Friends of the Earth — compressed geological time into the Genesis story, and he pointed out that it's not until the *final* day, at 4 PM, that dinosaurs first walk the earth. By 9 PM, all dinosaurs are extinct and redwoods sprout. It isn't until 11:57 on the last day that humans appear! At 11:59 and forty-five seconds Jesus is born."

De Graaf pauses. I try to absorb this timeline. "At one-fortieth of a second before midnight, the Industrial Revolution begins, and since then, we've used up most of the earth's resources and consumed more than all the rest of the people who ever lived. Here Brower famously said: 'There are people who think what we've been doing for the last fraction of a second can continue indefinitely. They are considered reasonable people, but they are stark raving mad!'"

These words — *stark raving mad* — echo through the courtyards even more forcefully than *humanity — obsessed by growth* did a moment before. Neither of us speaks. I'm perspiring. Tar Beach sweats, too. Morning dew slicks its silver coat, and our single tree, growing out of the tiny courtyard below into a flourishing canopy above, perspires in full-summer green. I look up at a pair of robins fluttering between branches; rusty blacktails, Blackburnian warblers, and Bicknell's thrush have also visited our Cornelia Street rooftop. De Graaf, too, has flown in from the West Coast, our first "tiny-house guest" — for a single night, then he goes to stay with a niece — and Melissa and I have woven him into our micro-waltz. (He sleeps on the only-room couch, and we use the roof for chats and a meal.) De Graaf is in New York at the invitation of Prime Minister Jigmi Thinley of Bhutan at the United Nations, part of a team of experts tasked to advise the prime minister on ways to adapt Bhutan's national policy of "gross national happiness," or GNH, elsewhere in the world.

Talk about Slow Policy. GNH, de Graaf explained to me the previous evening, seeks to dethrone gross domestic product. Whereas GDP measures just one thing — economic throughput — GNH guides the Bhutan's policies through measuring quality of life and social progress using nine indicators, including physical, mental, environmental, workplace, community, and political well-being. The very last of the nine indicators is economic. This more holistic and psychological approach led Bhutan, in a widely cited 2007 University of Leicester study, to be ranked eighth out of 178 countries in "subjective well-being." I ask de Graaf why he was selected to advise Bhutan.

"It has to do with something new we're doing in the Pacific Northwest," he says. In an animated voice, he describes the "municipal happiness surveys" he helped pioneer in Seattle. Adapting Bhutan's GNH model, de Graaf's group, along with others, conducted surveys to assess people's happiness. "The idea is to shape policy around what causes well-being, instead of simply ramping up economic growth. Our polling proves that, overwhelmingly, urban people finger stress and overwork as a grave problem. This suggests policies like four-day workweeks and stronger maternity leave to get our lives in equilibrium."

As he talks, I'm casually scanning the fire escape and tree for the baby doves. Melissa and I have been watching them each day, but no sign of them now. Could they have fledged?

"Through our GDP addiction," de Graaf goes on, "we're

maximizing the wrong things. BP spills oil, and GDP goes up because of the expensive cleanup. None of the environmental costs are factored in! And, on the social side, divorces rise and GDP rises...because of legal fees and selling the house." He squints toward a church clock-tower to the southeast. *Stark raving mad* echoes in my head. De Graaf says: "Well, I'm off to meet the prime minister."

TWO DAYS LATER, ON SUNDAY, I'm on the subway and over-hear a middle-aged woman complaining to her husband. "Pulling us onto the 6, honey?" she says, testily. "*Really?* But you know the 5's across the platform."

She's scowling. Her husband shrugs and looks away. Their young daughter — eight years old or so, with chestnut pigtails — ignores both of her parents, staring out the window as we race from 23rd Street to 14th.

Interestingly, the family is not exactly on the wrong train. Both the 5 and 6 do the same job. But the former is the "express," skipping several stops in this part of Manhattan. They'd shave a couple minutes off their trip by taking the 5.

"Get ready, honey," Mom says to her daughter, grabbing her arm. "We're getting off at the next stop to switch to the *express.*"

The girl twirls a pigtail. She looks up at her mom, then gazes back out the window where the steel pod we're in blasts through Middle Earth. "But Mommy," she says, "isn't *this* the express?"

Among those of us seated and standing close enough to overhear this conversation, smiles bloom. As happens sometimes in New York, I find myself snapped out of anonymity, unexpectedly exchanging knowing glances with strangers. Innocently, the girl surfaces a truth.

I detrain at 14th and climb the grungy concrete stairs into the sunlight. As strollers whiz by and taxis honk impatiently, I think of actress Carrie Fisher's quip that "these days even instant gratification takes too long." I take out my leather Bolivian notebook. I'm walking with a question this morning, but it's still unclear. I repocket the notebook.

Strolling west toward Union Square, I consider the family on the subway. Pace is relative. As we continually crank up life, the past year's tempo can feel tedious. But the little girl lives in a timelessness that eludes her harried parents. Like most adults, they are no doubt handcuffed to schedules. We even talk about being "time rich" or "time poor," as if time were a kind of currency to spend or hoard.

My Slow Year has been surfacing an alternative perspective. Before slowing down, I lived in a time-scarcity mentality, scheduling my life as tightly as possible and sometimes stressing about whether I was maximizing the utility of each meeting or social engagement. But now, I'm increasingly seeing the scarcity of time as artificial.

Arriving at Union Square, I walk into the largest farmers' market in America. In season, over 250,000 people shop for local farm products here each week. This is a good thing, of course. It slashes transport-carbon and promotes nutrition while growing the locavore food economy. But after witnessing here, one morning, a bidding war over the last bunch of organic basil, which nearly came to fisticuffs, Melissa and I more often go to the Sheridan Square farmers' market, with its twenty stalls and more flaneur pace.

Skirting the bustling Union Square market, I find a relatively quiet bench on the square's south side. I sit, take out my thermos of ginger tea and my notebook, and write: *Is there time?* Then I gaze up at the dizzying sight above: the Metronome.

Many New Yorkers mistake the iconic Metronome — a line of fifteen enormous orange LED numbers whirring by several stories up on the façade of One Union Square — for a countdown. It's actually a clock. Commissioned to artists in 1999, the Metronome works like this: The leftmost digits show the time in conventional twenty-four-hour format, displayed in hours, minutes, seconds, and tenths of a second. So, as "0945412" flashes by, it means that 9 hours, 45 minutes, 41 seconds, and 2/10 of a second have already passed today. The rightmost digits display the amount of time remaining in the day, also to a dizzying tenth of a second.

Under the Metronome, I loiter, sipping tea and reading Canadian journalist Carl Honoré's *In Praise of Slowness*. Measuring time, Honoré observes, is not new to our species. Some twenty thousand years ago, European Ice Age hunters marked the days between lunar phases by carving lines into bones. Since then, time's measurement has become increasingly precise. In 1500 BC came the Egyptian sundial. The thirteenth century brought the first crude mechanical clock in Europe. By the late seventeenth century, clocks evolved to measure not just hours but minutes and seconds, too.

The Industrial Revolution rewarded speed as never before, and the clock became its organizing instrument. "The clock," Honoré writes, "is the operating system of modern capitalism, the thing that makes everything else possible — meetings, deadlines, contracts, manufacturing processes, schedules, transport, working shifts." Social critic Lewis Mumford called the clock "the key machine" of the Industrial Revolution. But convincing the first industrial workers to abide by the clock was not easy. Many worked at their own speed, took breaks when they pleased, and often simply failed to show up.

"To teach workers the new time discipline demanded by modern capitalism," Honoré observes, "the ruling classes set about promoting punctuality as a civic duty and a moral virtue, while denigrating slowness and tardiness as cardinal sins." For example, the 1891 catalog of the Electric Signal Clock Company chastised those who failed to speed up: "If there is one virtue that should be cultivated more than any other by him who would succeed in life, it is punctuality." One of the company's clocks — called, rather ironically, "the Autocrat" — promised to "revolutionize stragglers and behind-time people."

The culture of hurry had worsened by nineteenth century's end. Proto-management consultant Frederick Taylor, for instance, at the Bethlehem Steel Works in Pennsylvania, used a slide rule and stopwatch to determine how long each task should take...to the fraction of a second. He then arranged tasks for maximum efficiency. "In the past, the man has been first," Taylor declared. "In the future, the System must be first."

I look up at the dizzying Metronome: 13 hours, 16 minutes, 11 seconds, and 6/10 of a second left this Sunday. *In the future, the System must be first.* Dawdling over Honoré and tea, I consider Taylor's prediction for another 6 minutes and 43 seconds, then saunter south down Broadway. On that brash boulevard, I look up and start "living at the third story," which is a Slow City practice Melissa and I have dreamed up.

living at the third story

Living at the third story challenges the street-level com-mandment that thou must ingest sample sale and fast food come-ons wholesale. I only need half my attention on the street, I have discovered, to keep from sleepwalking into traffic and other pedestrians. As the rest of my focus rises out of the buy-o-sphere and into the biosphere, I notice nut-brown oak branches and green leaves fluttering with white butterflies. An off-turquoise sky. Stretchy clouds. A devious gargoyle winking down at me from a portico.

As gridlock, taxi-top strip-club ads, and the crush of shop-pers gets backgrounded, my body relaxes. My new foreground: the ebony shine of a baby grand piano through an apartment window. And — *look!* — there's the bright white Washing-ton Square Arch capped with a red-tailed hawk, the sunlight gleaming on its wings.

It's Bobby, who nests atop an NYU administration build-ing, outside the university president's office window. A few

weeks back, William the Pigeon Guy pointed out Bobby to Melissa and me, and we've been tracking his movements. I walk into Washington Square Park and sit on the lawn, focused on the motionless raptor. Nobody else seems to notice him. I know from William that Bobby is "still-hunting," eyeing pigeon cutlets and mourning dove filets below.

Time passes. Or does it? Hawk-on-arch gazing, my mind drifts south to Bolivia and the indigenous Amazon Chiquitano people with whom I worked for several years. Their language has no word for future. My Chiquitano friends live in what sociologists call "natural time," where intuition and instinct guide action, not a schedule. Eat when hungry. Sleep when drowsy. Time, to the Chiquitanos, isn't an arrow flying from point A to B. It's a renewable resource, like the ocean's tide or the cooling Sur winds that blow up from Patagonia.

Union Square's Metronome would be incomprehensible to the Chiquitanos, and they aren't alone in this respect. On Canada's Baffin Island, the Inuit use the same word — *uvatiarru* — to mean both "past" and "future." In other philosophical traditions, ranging from Hindu to Buddhist, time goes, then it comes back. It's not scarce, as we've become conditioned to believe in today's society.

I'm aware of the Jam, center-square, grooving on the Temptations, but only peripherally. I'm slipping into the breeze in the leaves above, into the third story, into red-tail perception. Slipping into Natural Time. Bobby unself-consciously studies his prey. I wonder why this moment, right before an attack, doesn't feel violent. I recall a moment in South Africa's Kruger National Park, when I witnessed a lion take down a young female gazelle. In the final instant of the chase, after the gazelle tripped, she seemed to almost offer her neck into the lion's mouth generously, even sensuously. Fifty other gazelles in her pack jumped a creek and vanished. Gazelles continue.

Bobby takes wing.

He rises on a thermal coming off the hot asphalt, then alights on a tree limb. I stalk the west lawn, eyes on Bobby. All at once, the hawk sinks, anchor-like, toward a flock of pigeons feeding on a walkway. Lookout pigeons on the flock's perimeter release a cry-and-flutter that sends every pigeon airborne. Just before colliding with the pavement, Bobby curves into the avian rise and — using his talons — seizes a pigeon from the air. He wings the pigeon to a high oak bough, and I race toward him. At the base of the tree, out of breath, I look up. The pigeon no longer moves. The silhouette of William the Pigeon Guy moves toward me, along with a half dozen others who noticed the spectacle. Bobby crunches into bone, and feathers float down. I catch one.

FOR SEVERAL DAYS, I carry the blue-gray feather around the city. It feels like a soft bridge into Natural Time. I have it in hand when I meet John de Graaf for an early breakfast at Prodigy before his flight back to Seattle.

When I arrive, de Graaf looks up from one of the free issues of *The Onion* found in ubiquitous kiosks throughout the city. "Check out this headline," he says. "Perky 'Canada' Has Own Government, Laws." De Graaf chuckles.

"How's the prime minister?" I ask.

"Excellent. Gross national happiness could go gangbusters." De Graaf reports that some Pacific Island countries are already adopting versions of it — and are already seeing benefits like increased budget allocations for education and health, and reduced stress — and the UN is poised to declare an International Happiness Day. Prime Minister Thinley, de Graaf says, was intrigued to hear about Take Back Your Time Day, which is observed in America each year on October 24. If Americans lived in Western Europe, we would have already completed our work year by that date. On average, Americans work 350 hours — or nearly nine full weeks — longer than our European counterparts.

I show de Graaf the feather and tell him about living at the third story, about the Chiquitano concept of cyclical time. He gets up, returning with two mugs of steaming coffee. He places one in front of me and leans forward to smell the pair of flowers in a little vase on our table. "Bread and roses," de Graaf says. "That was an early-twentieth-century labor movement slogan in America. Workers put it on banners they hoisted at protests: 'We Want Bread...and Roses, Too!'"

I sip my coffee, waiting for him to elaborate. Out the window a hazy early morning light softens the buildings' edges, reminding me of a Hélder Câmara poem.

I was afraid
that with their blocks of concrete
   the skyscrapers might wound the dawn.

But you ought to see
how sensitive they are
to the morning light,
how they disarm
and lose their cutting edge.

De Graaf finally says: "The bread was good wages. And the roses? American workers were demanding *time*, in the form of shorter working hours." He picks up the pigeon feather from the table, examining both sides.

"Time to smell the roses?"

"Precisely. And the tragedy is that they didn't get it. We're working more than we were a generation ago. Without leisure, we're slaves. This is a freedom fight."

Before he goes, de Graaf tells me the story of a working-class mom who came up to him after one of his recent lectures. She and her husband have to each work full-time at retail jobs to keep up with the bills, and they lack decent benefits. They scrape to afford the childcare they need and are rarely with their children. "She was at the point of tears," de Graaf says, "like she was personally angry at me for not winning more work-life balance policies. And this is the richest country on the planet?"

After de Graaf leaves, I walk to the river. From Pier 45 I watch the Hudson's flow as the rising sun paints its ripples in pastels, the same flow Whitman watched, and Emerson, and Edward Abbey. *Time is a renewable resource*, I think, *but we're sold the idea it's scarce*. It's been stolen from that overworking mom and from almost everybody I know. I feel my fists clenching up. I'm confused and a little angry.

As I put some distance between myself and industrial time, I contemplate the David-and-Goliath battle underway today all around the globe. People like de Graaf and Jigmi Thinley put happiness first. Journalists like Honoré report on how American workers lost the roses. There's spiking interest in the international Slow Food movement and in decompression activities like Tai Chi, Tantric sex, and Slow Travel. In Austria each year, people gather from all over Europe in the town of Wagrain for the annual conference of the Society for Deceleration of Time, whose members explore pragmatic means of slowing down. In Japan, the Sloth Club advocates a less-hurried and more-harmonious lifestyle, and it has swollen to seven hundred members, part of a trend called the "Latinization of Japan." As Sloth Club cofounder Keibo Oiwa puts it: "More and more people in Japan, especially young people, are realizing that it is okay to be slow. For us, that represents a total sea change in attitudes."

But do these growing movements stand a chance against the Goliath of overwork?

TWO DAYS LATER, I'm far calmer. Melissa lays a loving gaze on me in the mauve 6 AM light coming through the window of our red-brick Soho yoga center: Golden Bridge NYC.

A dozen of us have just finished two hours of sunrise *sadhana* — the morning spiritual practice in the kundalini tradition — and we are still on our mats. This is the first time Melissa and I have been motivated to celebrate *sadhana*. We usually take Golden Bridge's evening classes, but we decided to try something different when, at 3:45 AM, we biked here for an intense hour of kundalini yoga postures, followed by another hour of meditation where, as the dawn swelled, we sang seven gorgeous mantras.

Between our mats, resting on the hardwood floor, is the pigeon feather. Melissa picks it up and strokes the back of my hand with it. I feel spacious, the morning practice programming me out of my looping thoughts. "There is something about embracing the day with the intimacy of a lover that makes one well again," writes Benedictine nun Macrina Wiederkehr when talking about the lauds, or morning prayer, at the cusp of day, her tradition's version of *sadhana.*

Our yoga teacher, Amanbir — a thirty-something black man in a white turban who has been leading *sadhana* from the front of the room — now stands up. He's six feet tall, slender, and exudes energy and peace. Melissa and I have often remarked that, in the three years we've taken yoga with Amanbir (we began attending his classes while still in Queens), we've not once seen anything other than joy in him. No visibly bad moods, stress, or impatience. Now, as he packs up the tablet computer he'd used to play the mantras, I realize that what I'm feeling — and what Melissa and I feel after Amanbir's evening Golden Bridge kundalini classes — is akin to Natural Time.

Could spiritual practice, particularly when it's intended to stop the mind and connect the practitioner with the present moment, be pointing toward the nonindustrialized consciousness of an Amazonian Chiquitano?

Manhattan bursts with temples and churches, ashrams and gudwaras. There are over two hundred yoga centers in the city. Many New Yorkers I know have some sort of spiritual practice. "I can't imagine living here without yoga" is how one friend put it to me. But I often experience yoga and meditation more as a kind of balm applied to the wound of overwork and time poverty. It helps me to put the petty troubles of life into a larger perspective, but a few hours of choked sidewalks and hard deadlines wears the yogic balm thin.

But these days, my life off the mat increasingly has a *sadhana* texture. I feel freer. I'm deliberately cultivating an ongoing Slow City consciousness of third-story gargoyles and

wonderful

red-tails and Natural Time. Perhaps it's true what neuroscientific data shows, that meditation forms new neural pathways, literally changing the brain in a positive way.

Silently, Melissa and I accompany Amanbir down the stairs. Out front on Centre Street, Melissa exudes praise about the morning practice. Amanbir nods, his eggshell-white turban a sharp contrast with his dark skin. It's 6:15 AM, and the car horns already echo down Centre. "What's your secret, Amanbir?" Melissa asks. "You never leave Manhattan, but you always seem so calm and centered."

Amanbir laughs. I hear a bit of de Graaf there. Both men have an Ekeko-lightness amid the city's craziness, and yet they could hardly be more different. As I wonder for a moment how their two strains of Natural Time — spiritual and practical — might dovetail together, Amanbir produces a tangerine from his backpack and begins to peel it. He breaks the peeled fruit into three sections, handing portions to Melissa and me.

I'm hungry. Triggered by the feel of fruit on my fingers, my mouth waters. "Feeling serene in the city," Amanbir says, looking at the bright orange fruit in his hand, "is often about what's right in front of you. For example...what's food to you?"

5. THE SLOWEST FOOD

NINE EATERIES NESTLE into our short Greenwich Village block — earning Cornelia Street the moniker Restaurant Row — and one of Cornelia's most fêted restaurants, Pearl Oyster Bar, is directly across from our horse entrance. In the evenings, fashionistas swoosh into Pearl — women with honeyed cascades of hair; men wearing platinum watches — but mornings bring the unassuming Juan and his delivery truck.

Hirsute and grinning, Juan unloads Styrofoam coolers of fresh rockfish, sea bass, and clams onto the sidewalk. When we coincide — usually I'm en route to Amy's Bread — I always stop to talk to him *en español*. Juan opens lids for my viewing, one of his gold-framed incisors often catching the morning sun as he chats about the catch. As I touch fish, up well memories from boyhood fishing on Long Island, where I used to hook baby bluefish from an estuary pier. New York dashes by as Juan and I idle over the salt-fish spoor of blue crab, eel, and fluke. It's a micro seaside getaway for me, and I can tell Juan enjoys the attention. It's part of something I've discovered: the reciprocity of Slow. A pause from *negotium* deflates facelessness. Juan, rooftop farmer Anastasia, William the Pigeon Guy, guitar-jamming Bruce — when we are seen and appreciated, the human connection inflates our mutual well-being.

One Wednesday morning, the horse gate clicks shut behind me and I hear a sharp whistle. Juan is beckoning me over. "Mañana," he whispers conspiratorially as we shake hands, "llevo los 'scallops' más fantásticos de Nueva York!" *Tomorrow night. The most fantastic scallops in New York.*

I'd already heard about Pearl's scallops. My foodie-friend Leon couldn't believe I lived steps away from the oyster bar and had yet to taste their scallops. Sure, he told me, Pearl's lobster rolls and tableside-filled grouper are exquisite, but nothing they serve compares to their seared scallops. When Leon said this, I thought of rushing over immediately, but I held back. I'd just read an article by psychologist Fred Bryant about the boon of anticipation. His research demonstrates that we feel good when we get something we want right away, but we feel better — a lot better, actually — when we look forward to something for a while and *then* get it. That's because not only do we get an itchy pleasure in imagining what we desire, but we also experience a huge spike in endorphins when a much-anticipated desire is fulfilled.

So I decided to test out a new Slow practice — "cultivating anticipation" — on Pearl, and I've been savoring the anticipation of Pearl's scallops for a fortnight, ever since Leon had told me about them. But now, with Juan's tip, I know it's time. Well, almost.

cultivating anticipation

Thirty hours. That's how much additional anticipation I get to cultivate until the following evening at Pearl, when "New York's most fantastic scallops" are served. As I clock in a solid two-hour workday on a *Washington Post* article, I imagine the sizzle of scallops in the background. I pedal five miles up the Hudson River bike path to the George Washington Bridge, picturing my scallops in a trawler passing beneath the bridge. That night, as a full moon rises, scallopesque, over Tar Beach, Melissa and I gaze into the glowing halo of Pearl on Cornelia below, imagining together the meal we will share. I fall asleep dreaming of the moment — before the moon doth rise tomorrow — of that virgin bite of a Pearl Oyster Bar scallop.

The next day, my tightly tweaked anticipation is momentarily undermined by a text from Melissa: she has to work late, but she insists I go without her. I push aside thoughts of our uni-moon days, grumble angrily at our work system — which is no friend to romance — and find myself alone, sipping chardonnay at one of the restaurant's close-placed two-tops. Finally, release is in view, and the waiter approaches. First, a hot buttery scent. Then I spy two bulging scallops beside roasted potatoes with truffle oil and a light salad. The plate is positioned before me.

Gazing at the dish, I silently recite the Buddhist saying that Melissa and I repeat aloud before meals at home to help bring us fully into the space of the food: *In this food we see clearly the presence of the entire universe supporting our existence.* Then I cut a communion sliver. I place it on my tongue.

How long do the dreamlike shapes of waiters dance? How long the orchestral sounds from Pearl's open kitchen, the weight of its stainless silver, the satiny feel of my napkin? Natural Time. Women's soft hair and men's wristwatches move through space, and the music is cool blues. As I savor the scallops, I understand in a new way a Buddhist saying — "When you eat, *eat*" — because I'm ecstatically absorbed.

When I finally finish, the waiter takes the plate and asks how it was. I'm mute and can manage no more than a grin. "Gotcha," he says.

Whilst I am in Scallopland, two thirty-something men in business suits sit at the table directly beside me. I overhear one order, yes, the scallops. Now, their plates arrive just after mine is removed, and the buttery scent of scallops wafts up once more.

I turn to tell the man he's ordered well, but I hesitate. On his plate, instead of two full-moon scallopy beauties, there is but one.

In the split second it takes me to process this, he saws into the remaining scallop — *Wait a minute…Is it possible that he already ate the first?* — forks it into his mouth, utters a sentence to his friend, swills wine, stabs the second half-moon, and steam-shovels it into his mouth.

Just like that, the scallops are gone.

WHAT'S FOOD TO YOU?

The next morning, a big summer sun rising over Tar Beach, I write Amanbir's question from post-*sadhana* Golden Bridge in my Bolivian notebook. I look up from the question, out over the fire escapes toward Pearl Oyster Bar. I know I have absurdly overfetishized Slow Scallops. Yes, it's wonderful to cultivate anticipation and great to savor food. But in the end, scallops are bivalve mollusks that use sticky mucus to trap their own larvae for dinner.

And yet. To my table neighbor, the scallops were invisible. He talked seamlessly through his Fast Scallops, through two drinks, and through a slurped-down flan while texting with others to coordinate movie plans. The pair felt like a mini-tornado whipping past. But the dining certainly loosened them up.

Melissa and I talk about food. It's a way, she says, of running her fingers along New York's texture. Eating out has always been our biggest splurge, and one we have carefully budgeted into our Slow Year. We savor Manhattan haute cuisine landmarks like candlelit Baobab, off Washington Square Park, for its black pasta with rock shrimp. Other times, we take the subway or our bikes to experience delightful Russian food dives in Brighton Beach, Nepalese under the thundering above-ground R train in Jackson Heights, or Oaxacan in Alphabet City. Eating connects us to our food shed. Since so many New York chefs — from Shawain Jay at Café Blossom on Carmine Street to Simpson Wong at Wong on Cornelia — are sensitive to serving "in season," we know it's summer when there's warm kale salad at Tartine, know it's fall when there's butternut squash at Home. In each locale, we delight over the changing menu's words, take our time in ordering, share dishes to maximize variety, and allow stretches of silence in the eating.

Alas, Manhattan loves food, but not slowly, even in the foodie-anointed restaurants. New York's hip bistros are loud with music and quick conversation. *Cultivate anticipation?* Could you translate that into American, please? The French practice of luxuriating in the subtle palate of a drawn-out meal is overshadowed by scallop-sawing. Socialize and tickle the innards, but don't draw breath before asking the most important question of all: what's next?

One afternoon, I'm at my bay-window table at Prodigy Coffee when a couple of lady foodistas sit down at the adjoining table.

"What's your favorite Micronesian sandwich in Midtown?" one of them, in oversized Louis Vuitton glasses, loudly asks.

My innards clench as they dissect the topic, exemplifying the baffling New York blend of food as status marker and social tool. Typically, food debates are as large as the stakes are miniscule, such as the ongoing craze over the best gastropub hamburger. "I spent two years perfecting my hamburger," one West Village chef once told me, with a flourish over his patty. "A thousand errors led to *this*."

After exhausting Micronesian sandwiches, the pair graduates to types of salt. Yes, salt. I've already heard this debate, which rages among New York chefs: is the Very Best Salt flake or coarse, fleur de sel or gale grosso, from Sicily or Uyuni? I'm increasingly irritated as I listen, and I realize it's because I recognize another New Yorker in them — yours truly. I'm uncomfortable imagining someone eavesdropping on my own foodie conversations. A fifty-something man wearing a bowtie seems even more irked. He shifts in his chair and stares their way, before turning to the pair. "Excuse me," he says to them, interrupting, "but have you been to Little Antarctica?"

"Little Antarctica?" Ms. Vuitton asks.

He nods. Both ladies lean toward him, eyes popping with interest, their minds evidently racing to what Antarctican food might be like. In the lull, I grasp that the guy is kidding — only sixty people live year-round on that continent, and they're all scientists subsisting on freeze-dried beets. Vuitton places her cappuccino cup down decisively and declares: "I'm so *there*!"

THE FOLLOWING WEEK, Melissa and I attend a benefit for the Brooklyn Food Coalition at some friends' brownstone in

Park Slope. Jeremy Scahill, author of *Blackwater*, has just delivered a tirade against corporate agriculture to the 150 people gathered, and Melissa and I now sit at a long table, eating buffet lasagna and local greens shoulder to shoulder with revolutionary Brooklynites. Melissa is practicing the Buddhist technique of chewing each bite thirty times before swallowing, in order to appreciate the food and better digest. It's a little comic to see her *tempo gusto* set against the speed-eating of the two broad-shouldered guys to her left and right. Both wear Portlandia-approved plaid — one sports a Che Guevara beret, complete with a red star — and they swill Brooklyn Lager and chow organic chard with a touch of scorn, openly maladjusted to bohemian-bourgeois (or "bobo") foodie elitism.

Following Melissa's example, I chew slowly, savoring the bites while observing the various approaches to food politics I'm witnessing. The first approach is that of "food-is-power" revolutionaries like the guy in the Che beret, a community organizer. He talks with his mouth full, ingesting calories quicker than you can say Fast Scallop. In some lefty circles, relishing food is counterrevolutionary. That's because — come global warming–induced droughts and floods and the demise of corporate agriculture — we'll all have to subsist on dandelion greens anyway.

Across from Che and company, in a circle of chairs, is another approach embodied by acolytes of a New York City Slow Food "convivium." Conviviums work like this: Slow Food members — under the premise that an unhurried pace of life begins at the table — gather at regular intervals to prepare and enjoy locally grown food. Conviviums blossomed out of the global Slow Food movement founded in 1986 by

Italian culinary writer Carlo Petrini, who led a protest against the opening of the first McDonald's in Rome. Since then, Slow Food has grown to eighty thousand members across 150 countries, and it includes over a thousand conviviums. *Time* magazine rated Slow Food as one of the eighty ideas that shakes the world.

Conviviums are wonderful community-building opportunities, and observing this group, I wonder again why Melissa and I haven't joined one. Previously, we'd chalked it up to not wanting to schedule an additional activity; we preferred living "slower food" more spontaneously in our daily lives. But while I appreciate the convivium, I also understand why the revolutionaries at our table disdain food fetishism, which I see so plainly in myself.

I finish eating, excuse myself, and walk out onto the back deck for air. The home's owners, our friends Lew Friedman and Nancy Romer, big-heartedly share their space with humanitarian groups. Melissa and I admire the couple immensely. Lew is a retired inner-city school teacher, now working for a union. Nancy is an industrious activist who successfully founded and led the Brooklyn Food Coalition, which has brought fresh, local food into city-school cafeterias and achieved "living wages" for food-industry workers. The pragmatic progressive efforts of people like Lew and Nancy, like de Graaf, like Brooklyn Grange's Anastasia — all embody yet a third approach. They stir up my pride in America and its potential to reinvent the culture and economy, even as these thoughts cast the Leisure Ethic I'm pursuing in a dubious light.

What's food to you? To Nancy and Lew, it's to be enjoyed and also leveraged for social justice. Shouldn't *that* be the model for me, of striving for social change the way they do, even if it means putting nose to grindstone every day?

"I'm confused," I say to Amanbir, outside Golden Bridge. We've just finished a particularly grueling hour-and-a-half kundalini yoga class, with twenty-minute "ego eradicator" arm holds.

"If you're not confused, you're fused," Amanbir replies. His turban is crisp-white against the faded gray of the Old Police Headquarters — now converted to high-end apartments — on Centre Street. Chinatown's apartments rise in a jumble to the south. My mind tries to unravel this. *Confused*: open, questioning. *Fused*: dogmatic, stuck.

I remind Amanbir of his question to us about food. Very un-yogicly, I rant that food is too many darn things. It's social change, status marker, and escapism. It's running your fingers along New York's texture. It's something to alternatively savor and disdain. I blurt out, finally: "Can't food just be *food*?"

Amanbir, exuding calm, seems to almost float a few millimeters above the asphalt. He reaches over and touches my forehead. "You're too much up here." Then he moves his hand, slowly, down to my fourth chakra. The heart. "Go in there and ask the question."

PALM BUTTER.

I ask the question, and the answer is palm butter.

It's the national dish of Liberia — an orange-red stew of savory palm oil and meat over pounded cassava. I ate it once in the rural town of Buchanan, Liberia, during the civil war. I was just placed under severe Level IV "hunker down" orders and knew it could be my very last meal.

That was back in 2001. Dictator Charles Taylor's grip on power was slipping as various rebel groups seized upcountry towns. As a fresh-faced aid worker with an American nonprofit based in the capital, Monrovia, I was among a handful of foreigners traveling to the country's most dangerous corners. My job was to distribute corn-soy blend, bulgur wheat, and vegetable oil to health clinics and orphanages. Our security officer had just radioed in the bad news — firefights in Monrovia — and announced the Level IV. Then the radio went silent. Dead. As I ate palm butter out of a communal wooden bowl with a trio of Liberian coworkers, I felt frightened.

Spooning the golden-red butter into our mouths, we spoke little. Was anarchy coming? Cell phones and landlines alike were nonexistent in war-torn Liberia, and still no radio. The week before, while in the country's north, outside the town of Gbanga near rebel lines, I saw a chilling bit of graffiti scrawled on the shell of a health clinic, which had been stripped of its tin roof and gutted of its beds. "The difference between war and peace," the graffiti read, "is two days without food."

"Little Liberia," I say to Melissa one night. We're stargazing on a blanket on Tar Beach. "I want to go there. To try and find palm butter."

She turns her head to me and smirks. "Just past Little Antarctica, right?"

I shake my head. "It's deep in Staten Island someplace. Some ten thousand Liberians settled there during the war. They got asylum under President Clinton, and it kept getting renewed. Now many have naturalized." I heard about it from a Liberian friend back in Monrovia who had relatives there, but the place feels a little mythical to me, even impossible. " 'Small Liberia' is what they actually call it."

Melissa giggles. "That's cute. Like 'tryin' small.'"

I've taught Melissa a smattering of Liberian English, and we sometimes slip into it. "Wait small, bosslady," I say.

She sits up. "Let's eat, bossman?" she pleads, eyes blinking theatrically. "I wan' eat palm butter in Small Liberia."

IT'S NOT EASY to get to New York's Small Liberia. You can't just hop the R. Melissa and I pedal the Hudson River bike path to the Staten Island ferry terminal. After security dogs sniff our bikes and pack, we board. "If you haven't got a nickel, it's the Staten Island Ferry," Bob Dylan crooned in the 1968 tune "Hard Times in New York Town," and the six-mile boat ride is still free today. We climb to the top deck, where the sky is a blue lens over the Statue of Liberty. As we steam past it, I think of my grandparents passing this spot in the 1920s when emigrating from Ireland — their names, William and Delia Powers, are etched on a plaque on Ellis Island, where they first landed. Today, a thousand of us ride a mighty orange vessel — tourists snapping photos, locals with jaded expressions, all traveling for free in full-chested, ferry-powered American freedom. Then all at once Melissa and I are biking out of the hull and up Staten Island's most brutal hill.

Melissa toughs it out in the lead on her 1960s white Tourist Expert IV ($35 used); me behind her on my 1970s yellow Iverson ($25 used). Our NYC bike map shows a "future bike lane" here, so we thought there would at least be a shoulder, but perhaps they meant a bike lane in *uvatiarru* — the Inuit distant past/future — because there's no trace of bike-friendliness. Hummers and Corvettes bear down on us. I hit a pothole and the Iverson swerves toward a barreling UPS truck. Melissa, out of breath, insists we stop.

I look over my shoulder and back down the hill. It would be easy to coast back down, maybe hit Staten Island's public beach. But my mind flashes back. Back to Liberia.

Level IV in Buchanan. Gunfire in the capital. Radio silence. By the last bites of palm butter, my fear had vanished. Food is death. Dead animal and plant matter. My own death is inevitable, and maybe today. "Thank God for life," my friend Sammalou, a Food for Peace field worker, said to me as we scraped our communal bowl clean.

A delivery truck belches black soot as it passes us on the Staten Island hill. Melissa coughs and looks longingly down the hill. "Are you sure there's even a restaurant in Small Liberia?" she says.

"Ten thousand Liberians live there. So there must be butter." I focus on the distant top of the hill. *Thank God for life.* "Let's try small."

I take the lead. Cultivating anticipation with each pedal-pump, I imagine a steaming bowl of palm butter. The mecca nears. The hill's summit lies just fifty yards above. I look back; Melissa's struggling. When the United States founded Liberia in 1822 as a homeland for freed American slaves, President James Monroe — Monrovia's namesake — described Liberia as "a little America, destined to shine gem-like in the heart of darkest Africa." Drenched in sweat, I picture the Small Liberia we are about to see as destined to shine, gem-like, in darkest Staten Island — a mangrove-embraced mini-Monrovia.

At last we reach the pinnacle, gasping for breath, but that's not what we see. No funky, Leisure Ethic–infused and half-collapsed outdoor discos serving Club Beer. No hips swaying to Ivorian *mapouka* like they do in Liberia's capital. There are neither chimpanzee islands nor colorfully clad women with straw baskets of cassava and boni fish on their heads.

From our hard-won peak, we gaze out over a massive Home Depot shining box-like through a haze of car exhaust. And beyond the asphalt savanna of a parking lot, below an expressway river, lies Small Liberia: a dozen identical housing-project apartment buildings.

Dejected, Melissa nevertheless queries a passerby, but he only frowns and says: "*Libyan* food?"

"*Liberian*," she says. "West African."

The man shrugs and indicates a Burger King beyond the Home Depot.

We attempt to bike down to the apartment buildings. But we keep hitting dead ends and have to double back again and again. Sunburned and frustrated, we finally wheel into a collage of parking lots, brick high-rises, concrete walkways, and more parking lots. Small Liberia.

Go in there, and ask the question. This is what Amanbir told me outside Golden Bridge. I went into my heart and asked, and I thought somebody said palm butter. Perhaps I misheard.

"Turn around, boss?" Melissa asks.

I'm about to agree. But then I notice something. A pulse.

Partly hidden behind a stand of trees beside one of the Soviet-reminiscent apartments are several dozen...*idlers*.

As we bike toward them, my heart hits a fresh clip. It looks like a Monrovia street scene. I smell the scent of "cow meat" rising from a makeshift grill. I hear South African music coming from somebody's radio. *Liberians!* Liberians lounging in beach chairs and standing in clusters of three or four, chatting. I get off my bike. Unable to contain myself, I approach the first man I see and introduce myself. "Flomo," he says as we clasp hands. I execute the national snap-handshake with Flomo.

"Hey, white man knows our Liberian ways!" he shouts.

In no time, a dozen men and women encircle Melissa and me, and the sound of popcorn popping fills the air as they school Melissa in the art: an ordinary hand clasp, followed by a mutual finger-slide. Let your middle finger catch firmly on theirs and out pops a satisfying mutual snap.

One of them is from Greenville. Another from Kakata. I've been to their hometowns, and we connect around a mutual love for Liberia. After a while, Melissa says, "I hungry-o!" Flomo produces a cell phone from his jeans pocket and dials his friend Precious. We lock bikes and follow Flomo to Building 6, Apartment 522, where he introduces us to the two women inside — the sixty-year-old Precious and her niece Kebeh. They invite us into the living room. "Got palava sauce," Precious tells us.

I'm still taking in the ambiance. There's a single poster on the wall behind Precious: "Barack Obama: First Black President of the United States." It's the simple décor and furniture of a Monrovia apartment. Everything functional, nothing fancy or excessive.

"Anything else?" I ask.

"Got palm butter with fufu," she says.

Five minutes later, Precious places a shared bowl before us. Melissa and I sink spoons into a golden sauce, drenching chunks of cow meat and pounded-yucca "fufu" paste. Melissa says she's never tasted anything so delicious and fulfilling. And I'm emotionally back in Buchanan, the capital secured again, alive to digest another day. Precious and Kebeh, noticing how much we're enjoying their creation, can't hide their pride.

What's food to you? It strikes me that food is nothing less than love.

Food is love. That's what's in my heart when, after a few hours with our new Liberian friends, Melissa and I coast effortlessly down the hill from Small Liberia to the Staten Island ferry terminal, board the boat just after sunset, and sail into Manhattan's million lights. Each light is a dish — Liberian palm butter and Salvadorian *pupusa*; Polish knish and my Nana's hot Irish soda bread — and each dish is an expression of home, the one left behind and the one we're creating together, now, in a city as strong and diverse as it gets. *Look*, Melissa says, *the Freedom Tower's grown a story or two*. We ride into its lights toward others: Washington Square Park, Cornelia Street, Pearl, the sole tree above Tar Beach. Home.

6. URBAN FERAL

ON A ROUTINE IMPROMPTU AFTERNOON, I dip into a sustainable cities panel at Columbia University. Architects and landscape planners imagine aloud a New York that combines the texture of the past with green technology and "permaculture" (a contraction of both *permanent agriculture* and *permanent culture*), so that Manhattan's concrete boundaries are replaced by wetlands and beaches for bird watching, riverside strolls, and sunbathing. "It's not just an aesthetic win," one of the panelists declares. "Renaturing the city's edge will protect it from climate change–induced 'storm surges' that could flood us out." Another panelist explains that, two years back, the top federal team of climatologists and engineers on emergency preparedness informed Mayor Bloomberg that the city must protect itself from these potential "storm surges," and they recommended the construction of dikes off New York Harbor. The price tag for that massive project: $100 billion (money the city doesn't have). Its timeframe: decades (time the city doesn't have).

But for about a tenth of the cost and the time, New York could let its banks go pleasantly funky, and should the waters rise, those green spaces would absorb much of the flooding, sparing buildings and subways. The panelist shows a rendering of what it would look like. The image fascinates me. Back at the apartment, I sketch a version of it with Melissa's colored pencils and tack it above our fireplace.

When Melissa comes home that night, she studies it. "Cool," she says, "but there's something else, something that's already here in Manhattan today." Out the window our tree

scratches a branch against the fire escape; its leaves sweep the bedroom window. "It's part of how I find sanity in Manhattan: urban sanctuaries."

Fireworks flash and gongs sound. *Urban sanctuary!* This is a Slow City tool Melissa and I have both been using but didn't have the words for yet. While making dinner, we list our favorite urban sanctuaries. She gushes about Central Park's Ramble — with its circuitous paths looping down past waterfalls and pine groves — and the Tudor City gardens perched above First Avenue and 40th Street, an oasis to which she flees from her Midtown office to eat brown-bag lunches amid birdsong. My favorite sanctuaries: Pier 45's tip, where the West Side Highway fades to a hum; a back seat in the cathedral of St. John the Divine in late afternoon; the High Line, a new park sanctuary created from unused urban infrastructure; a silent, little-touristed third-floor corner of the Met reached via a concealed stairway in the Asian wing (it houses imaginative Chinese decorative arts).

Moongazing on Tar Beach after dinner, we muse on two other urban sanctuaries: Washington Square and Madison Square Parks on warm days, when we love to kick off sandals and lie back to savor that sensual press of our bodies to the Earth. Gravity's eros. I can feel that attraction now — and it's mutual, since our bodies exert a tiny gravity on the Earth — as my wife and I touch hands, the Milky Way invisible against Manhattan's illumination, with only Venus, the moon, and a handful of stars perforating through. I breathe deeply, remembering a new term my friend, the cultural ecologist David Abram, coined in his book *Becoming Animal*: Eairth. The word suggests that air isn't *above* the Earth, as we normally imagine, but inherent to it. "We live in the Earth — or the E*air*th — not on it," he told me once. The atmosphere around us is an ever-accessible urban sanctuary.

So is water. One Saturday afternoon, Melissa spots a sign along the Hudson bike path: "Free Kayaking." An arrow points up Pier 40, and we follow it. There's no catch. The nonprofit, all-volunteer Downtown Boathouse offers open-topped, double and single kayaks for nothing on weekends and Wednesday afternoons. We pull on life jackets, hop into two singles, and paddle through a delineated square of the river. As the kayak skims the glassy surface, droplets cool my forearms, and the lapping sound calms me. We stop to rest where a half dozen private sailboats are moored, imagining the navy-blue, thirty-two-footer beside us is ours.

"Manhattan!" I exclaim.

"Five days sail from Nova Scotia," Melissa says, "and now for some good food at last."

Leaning back in the kayaks, feet dangling into the water, we look up into the Eairth's blue and riff for a quarter hour on the adventures in "our" navy-blue sailboat. Momentarily, other adventures we've been talking about bubble up in my mind — a niggling sense of greater obligations within our marriage looming on the horizon — but I don't let these thoughts pierce the lightness of our joint daydream.

Our spontaneous boating fantasy heightens the sense of urban sanctuary. My body softens and my psyche de-stresses. When we eventually paddle back to the dock, our shorts are soaked and we're fully refreshed for asphalt reentry.

"How can this be *free*?" I ask a volunteer, who tells me it's part of the Downtown Boathouse mission to "create a constituency around kayaking that will one day force the city to renature Manhattan's boundaries for kayaking.... Now we only have access in this little square of water, and most of the city's edges are concrete, and there's no banks to launch a kayak from. So I guess we're a bunch of aquatic subversives."

It seems a long way from my soaked shorts to this vision. Nevertheless, the experience gets me dreaming, and back at the micro, I add a dozen colorful kayaks into the downtown marshes on the Natural City drawing.

THE FOLLOWING SLOW TUESDAY, I awake, descend the five flights, whistle my way through the courtyard and horse entrance, view the day's catch with Juan outside Pearl Oyster Bar, and then tote a still-warm Tuscan loaf from Amy's Bread to one of my favorite New York urban sanctuaries: St. Luke's Gardens on Hudson Street.

This alcove, a few blocks from Cornelia, harbors a hundred varieties of trees, shrubs, and flowers amid pleasantly circular paths and a scattering of benches. It's no Yellowstone — more the size of a suburban backyard — but St. Luke's is open to the public and little trod. I read Bashō's haikus, munch warm bread, and watch a dozen starlings gather breakfast. A few people hasten by, using the garden as a shortcut between appointments, but otherwise I'm alone. Before long, however, St. Luke's overripens with the growing noise of grinding bus brakes and whining Hudson River tourist helicopters. Townhouse backsides and the hulking seven-story apartment building on Greenwich Street thrust into the gardens. Lest one forget the "urban" in this sanctuary.

Knowing it's time for a switch-up, I amble to Prodigy,

fixing half my attention three stories up in the Eairth. Pigeon flocks do their double-helix trick. Rainbow prisms enliven an ancient chandelier in someone's living room. I enter Prodigy to the tart scent of ground espresso and the hiss of foaming milk. I order a cappuccino — the barista knows I take it "dry and extra hot" — and sink into my bay-window seat up front. I tuck into the marvelous foam and gaze out across the street where Unoppressive, Non-Imperialist Bargain Books (yes, that's its name) nudges into Wisdom of Tibet: Spiritual Goods. In the Village, it seems, politics lies south of religion, and both take plastic.

I feel blessed. Before I got up this morning, Melissa had already hand-drawn a birthday card for my mother. Then she came into the bed to cuddle, and I'm sipping into those cuddles now. We both recognize our overall happiness has increased since the move to Manhattan. Beyond the pleasure of staycations, kayaking, and Little Liberia, the very act of dreaming up a fresh vision for our life and implementing it together creates a bond. Yet right now a streak of guilt washes through my joy, guilt over getting to do so much of nothing so often while she works. That guilt is mixed with a touch of loneliness; my stepping into five-day weekends leaves me alone a lot of the time...and out of sync with Melissa. Whether it's eating scallops alone or idling in Prodigy, I feel isolated. I'm finding it hard to stake out a claim to stillness — if just for a few hours a day — in a place where everything always moves.

"Don't do. *Be*." I recall Jackie's words from the 12 x 12 and realize a lot of what's been making me come most alive has nothing to do with the ambition and achievement that used to fuel me. It's the very simple things: chatting with Juan over striped bass, singing with Bruce and the Jam, feeding almonds to a pigeon with William, savoring Precious's palm butter in Small Liberia. Sip from each little stream, mutually nourish, kindle a slower city. Who says one has to go hermit and steal away to Bashō's blue mountain? John Milton wrote: "They also serve who only stand and wait." Here, in Manhattan, I feel the heat of my mug, breathe café scents, and I simply look.

Out Prodigy's window, beside Unoppressive, Non-Imperialist Bargain Books, is a rainbow peppercorn of dreams. The scarlet Lee Noodle Bar, the lemon-yellow Pizza from Naples, a chartreuse Village Shoe Repair, and the weathered bricks of an old public pocket park, Downing Street Playground. From the playground's cornice flaps, gently, an American flag, and, in my imagination, its blue and red bleach to white, like Jasper Johns's "White Flag."

At the Met several days back I stopped in front of "White Flag," Johns's painting of the stars-and-stripes drained of color. I stood a long while admiring the beige and pearl-white stars and stripes, reading bits of newsprint textured into the white flag. By radically altering the flag's colors, he helps us see them. Johns's piece spoke to me about my work-a-day existence before leaving Queens. Whereas last year I'd look at a hundred flags and see none, now — by radically altering my days — each flag flares bright. New York flares bright. Slowing down, for me, bleached out Central Park and Wall Street, bleached Hudson and East, exposed the city's bones, so I might see, afresh, *de colores*.

The Downing Street Playground flag catches wind. Snapping south, the flag's whites flood blood red and ocean blue. People stride beneath it in forwardness and fashion, holding onto hats in the gust, clutching coffee-to-go. One harried gent

— tall, fiftyish, desk jockey–clad — notices the incongruity of another man treasonously idling in a bay window. Midstride, he glances up at the Prodigy sign, then back at me — curiosity on his face, his pace slowing a hair.

Then he disappears down the block, and my gaze shifts into the coffee shop, where the to-go line is forty-legs strong. Folks pay through smarties via Square. A hipster arrives at the tablet-computer cash register and says: "Latte with five shots." The barista responds: "One latte with five shots: $10.25 please."

Nine others sit at tables around, all engrossed in either laptops, tablets, or phones, most sprouting earbuds, and one — a dirty-blonde, late-twenties woman across from me — chooses all of the above. A spaghetti of wires tether her to the wall. She only stops typing on the laptop to respond to the chirp of incoming texts or write notes, in ballpoint pen, on the back of her hand. Manila folders and a weekly planner crowd her lap. For a moment, in my reverie, I feel light-headed, as if I'm suddenly on a strange planet, and at once bewildered and fascinated. Her forehead in knots, she talks on the phone while simultaneously typing. Then it strikes me: I'm looking at myself, less than a year ago.

This is momentarily consoling — for I've managed to extract myself from the busyness around me — but the solace is fleeting. All the multitasking around me shines a harsh light on my zero-tasking. I feel the White Flag sublimity and the blue mountain of Carmine Street dissipate. As my inner peace dissolves, into the vacuum tromps a cocky acquaintance.

So, Billy, the acquaintance says, *staring mindlessly at flags all morning, are ye now?*

Meet Monkey Mind. MM for short. He speaks to me in an Irish brogue.

Yes, I tell him. But flag-staring is mind*ful*.

MM chuckles. *You reap what you sow. Sow sloth-seeds on five-day weekends, and you'll harvest Failure.*

When I hesitate in responding, MM croons: *Why does everyone dart hither and thither with to-go cups? For their health? Aye! Their wealth-building-health, their status-health, their not-being-a-looney health!*

I take out the bagel I've snuck into Prodigy, bite into it, and willfully chew thirty times whilst patiently explaining to MM that I've 80/20'ed my week. I crushed my article, I tell him, and pounded out emails to earn this reverse weekend.

Aye, "crushed" and "pounded out" makes it sound like you're doing more than sitting on your arse.

But, I insist to MM, it's healthy to simply *look* for a few hours a day.

MM, that smoothie, responds in song, to the tune of "When Irish Eyes are Smiling": *Crush more articles / and you could win a Pulitzer! / Cradle your laptop / not a silly coffee mug / and you'll conquer the world.*

Double-M can carry a tune, but I've had enough of him. I leave Prodigy Coffee and fast walk a packed Sixth Avenue to Washington Square Park. MM's voice eventually decrescendos from *forte* to *pianissimo*. In his place, the sound of the Jam, minus Bruce today, riffing on something wordless and bluesy. Above, oaks and pines sway, and gradually my mind begins to open back up. I take out my Bolivian notebook and write: *The Natural City.*

My pen begins to sketch in the notebook. At first it's a

tiny version of the Natural City image above our fireplace. But I quickly realize that greening the edges of Manhattan isn't a deep enough reset. The voice of commerce — and how it reinforces competitive MM in me — is too strong. Joseph Campbell said: "If you don't like the culture, create your own." Don't like the boundaries of a city? Create your own.

Music plays, trees sway, and the city goes elastic under my pen. I draw a Manhattan Island segueing into the Catskills, into the great Adirondack State Park and its two million acres of lush mountains, lakes, and rivers that provides the city's watershed. Could such a "ripple city" transcend the current concept of metropolis through de Graafian work-life balance policies and twenty-first-century technologies? I imagine light-rails and electric cars moving people smoothly from the concrete core of this new city to its wilderness periphery. Job-sharing and expanded vacation leave liberate time for enjoyment of nature and spontaneous experience. Beyond uptown and downtown, there's Slowtown.

MELISSA AND I TAKE A SHORTLINE BUS to Slowtown, ripple-city north: Adirondack State Park. We depart Port Authority on a Friday afternoon and spend two nights with friends at their cabin on Lake George. Then Melissa buses it back for the workweek, and I hitch to a trailhead and hike into the park, planning to backpack in the woods for five nights. I wish Melissa could join me, but because of her job, she can't. A backcountry solo trip is second best.

I arrive Sunday evening, just as the weekend campers are leaving. "Where you headed?" an eager couple asks me at the trailhead. "Don't know," I tell them, and I don't. My goal is to leave Metronomes and MM behind. I want to be.

Adirondacks

And that's what happens. I pitch my tent on a remote Pharaoh Lake peninsula, cook my meals, sleep as much as I wish, bathe in streams and the lake, wander, and see not a tool-maker for the first two days. Then I hike ten miles deeper, camping for another three nights on a smaller lake higher in the mountains. My camping mattress punctures, and from then on I sleep right on the Earth, and that's fine. The profound silence is pierced occasionally by a coyote howl, the call of a moose wading on the far edge of the lake, the swoop and cry of five loons elegantly circling over the course of an hour, one by one down into the lake, sending off concentric circles that deliver ripples all the way to my legs, which dip from a boulder into the water, the leg hairs nibbled upon by phosphorescent minnows. At night, crawdads come out en masse, and I stare into their otherworldly eyes with the aid of my headlamp, as a beaver slaps his tail and a distant owl hoots.

MM is in the forest with me, of course, but I find my mind becomes as wide and clear as Pharaoh Lake, so I see the loops, spins, and dodges of monkey mind so much more clearly than in civilization. Amanbir's self-observation-without-judgment is so much easier here. The mind becomes my tool. I'm no longer its fool.

I'm a creature among creatures, living John Hay's "elemental life" of lake and rock and stream, and quite happily, I don't matter. I love the unexceptionality of humans out here. Neither jay nor elk gives a darn about the likes of me, and there's no "self" reflected back in billboards and Internet pop-up ads. No need for third-story living or urban sanctuaries. No need to pore over Abram's *Becoming Animal*. I'm animal.

Friday comes, by the marks in my Bolivian notebook, and though I hardly wish to leave this ripple-city periphery, I have to return to the core, to Melissa, for the truncated two-day weekend we get to share. So I hike the final eight miles out to the opposite side from where I entered and hitch a ride to Ticonderoga to catch the Amtrak back. The train parallels the Hudson to Grand Central Station, and then it's the familiar A train to West 4th and Cornelia.

THE APARTMENT SEEMS SMALLER. Sweeping Adirondack views narrow to the brick walls and fire escapes out each tiny window. Melissa and I decide to walk, holding hands down to the end of Pier 45. I gaze out at the light green Statue of Liberty and over to the Freedom Tower rising ever-higher toward completion, feeling the wilderness flowing down the Hudson to me. Instinctively, I pull off my sandals, thread through the pier's guardrail and onto a pylon.

I'm aware Melissa isn't following my lead. There's no sign, but it's an unspoken rule that you don't touch water here. Feet dangling from the pylon, the lapping water cooling my ankles, a kind of Pharaoh Lake peace overcomes any anxiety over bending this rule.

My eyes scan for "animalized water" — as Thoreau called fish in *Walden* — and notice the breeze sizzling the surface like flint sparking. I notice how the Statue of Liberty, Staten Island, and the Hoboken docks take on a humbler tinge from the cave-like intimacy below the pier. How much time passes? Five minutes? Ten?

"Come on, Melissa!" I say, over my shoulder. "Shed those shoes and get down here."

She glances backward, nervously, her hair doing a little wind dance. "I don't know," she says. "This isn't the Adirondacks."

Quizzical and perturbed stares come from folks Lady Liberty–gazing above me. Then Melissa's sharp voice slices down. "Police!"

Lizard brain activates. *Fight, flight, or freeze?* I flee, through the handrail bars. I notice an NYC Park Police SUV racing up the pier toward us, and I fall into stride with Melissa on a path away from the crime scene.

"Hold it!"

I stop and turn around. Two cops, male and female. The latter has her hand inches below the weapon on her belt, and she looks ready to seize it. "I think *I* know who it might have been," she says, staring at me hard.

Evidence abounds. Sandals dangle from my hand, dozens of eyewitnesses. My mind tabulates that I broke the law, probably by "trespassing" and "putting myself in danger."

Luckily, my feet aren't telltale wet. Just before fleeing, I'd been airing them above the water's surface. Then, in a kind of diffusion of focus, the police turn their heads to survey the other hundred people in the area. Several are also barefoot. As the police look around, Melissa and I turn and walk away.

With each step my back heats up a degree. I expect the weight of a police hand on my shoulder. *Will the person who phoned in the infraction snitch? Or was it a surveillance camera?*

The city, however, absorbs. In minutes, we've melted into the crowd and are gone.

Not two days later, I receive another scolding over proper habitat.

I'm downtown, having just tried out Occupy Yoga, a free daily kundalini yoga class in the 55 Wall Street atrium, a couple blocks from Zuccotti Park. It's one of dozens of outgrowths of the previous year's Occupy Wall Street phenomenon. After an hour of breath-of-fire and ego-eradicators, I stroll downtown joyfully at first, but I soon find the crush of suits and skyscrapers eat the peace. To keep my energy up, I walk into City Hall Park, but it's swollen with people. I spy one scrap of lawn, a kind of crabgrass welcome mat, but it lies behind a knee-high rope barrier.

I cross it onto dewy grass, longing to shed shoes, and step over to a gorgeous maple tree, but as I reach to touch its bark, an NYPD officer yells: "Hey!"

This man seems even more heavy-duty than the Pier 45 duo. He's evidently guarding a municipal building some thirty yards away — and this patch of lawn is part of the buffer.

"Can't you see the barrier?!"

My indignation swells. *You can't touch a tree in New York?* The officer looks outraged. The weaker animal, I turn and leave, soon back on concrete, unpursued.

I leave Manhattan, riding the A train into Brooklyn, amazed that I didn't notice the city's restrictiveness before. I wonder, too, what it does to everyone's psyche to live in this shadow of discipline, to live so separated from the natural sanctuary that feels so vital to being happy and alive. In Brooklyn, I reach my destination: a narrow slice of natural East River in Williamsburg, where water laps up onto an actual stony beach in a small park. But I'm barely out onto one of the small boulders just into the water when a young park worker approaches me. He's very polite. "Sorry, man," he says, "but you need to get off that rock."

"Why?"

"It's the rules. You could hurt yourself."

I remain on the rock. He chills on the beach, ten feet away. He's patient, cool. Brooklyn. The rest of Williamsburg to the north and south along the East River is high-rises and concrete docks. This rock is it. A kind of last stand.

I think of the drawing above our Cornelia fireplace. *The natural city?* After my recent run-ins, nothing could feel more far-fetched. While wilderness camping the previous week, I occasionally fantasized about abandoning New York and losing myself in wilderness for a lifetime. That desire returns under the man's disciplining gaze. I look away, standing firm, and glimpse Governor's Island beyond the Brooklyn Bridge. Out there, New York Harbor opens to the Rockaway peninsula. *Opens to the ocean.*

"You need to get off that rock," the parks employee repeats. "Sorry, man." New York has turned its back on the sea, but must I?

I return the guy's gaze. He'll wait all day. Or until somebody armed arrives. So I obey, stepping back to shore.

"WATCH MY STUFF A SEC?"

I lock eyes with a stunning Latina woman standing below my perch on a vacant Rockaway Beach lifeguard chair. She strips off her clothes down to a forest-green one-piece bathing suit.

"Of course," I manage to croak, whilst reorienting myself to the present moment. Waves crash on the beach; rose-colored sunset; the twenty-four-ounce beer I've been drinking; the hard copy of a piece for the *Atlantic* I'm revising. Yes, I'm working, even here. MM found a loophole in the five-day weekend: no laptop means no work. *As long as it's by hand, it's fun!* he sang.

So I've compromised: I decide to allow work to slide into leisure time as long as I neither use technology nor exceed two days (or sixteen hours) per week of work.

The young woman, who looks to be in her late twenties, pulls her long hair back in a bun and nods toward the pages in my lap. "Poetry?" she speculates.

"A piece for the *Atlantic*," I say.

"The Atlantic's right here," she replies, nodding out to the ocean. She explains about how she loves night swims, but "*that* guy" — she means the heavyset NYC parks official in an all-terrain vehicle who patrols the beach after 6 PM when the lifeguards pack up — has been pestering her all week.

The ATV zooms past, and she squats down, pretending to rifle through her bag, presumably so the parks official won't notice her. I ask her if she lives here.

She nods from her squat. "I pay practically zero for a little room. I trim medical marijuana for the state of Colorado three months a year and hang for nine." Other tidbits quickly surface: She's from Fort Collins, Colorado; parents born in Mexico, came here illegally before she was born; and dropped out of Western State University ("aka 'Wasted State' because of all the weed") before finishing her psychology thesis. Now she divides her New York time "between town and ocean."

Then, without a word, she's off. I take a long sip of beer. She's got a single visible tattoo — an Aztec-looking sun blazing on her right shoulder blade. She wades into the wave caps and dives under the surf.

I drain my beer and bury the notebook in my pack — I'm feeling buzzed, light, and productive from revising my article. I realize I'm done here, and Melissa will be home soon, but I've agreed to watch this person's belongings.

I see her body surface far beyond the break, dolphin-like, glistening. She floats for a while, then sidestrokes toward the break. As I wait, my mind wanders to a big decision Melissa and I took not long ago. We'd talked about it forever before doing anything, and though I feel good about it, uncomfortable questions keep coming up. I'm talking about our decision to stop using birth control.

Melissa and I have discussed children many times since our "Queens mama" reverie, and we've agreed we want to have a child together... someday. Then, right after the move to Manhattan, we decided the time had come. Now I wonder: What would it *really* be like to have a baby in Manhattan, to layer urban parenting into Slow? Today's spur-of-the-moment trip to the Rockaways would hardly be possible. Blue Bottle Coffee on the boardwalk. Scanning the ocean for dolphins. (I spotted none.) Eating Rockaway Tacos under the shade of the boardwalk. Walking the surf line for sea glass. Meeting this intriguing person who swims at sunset.

How beautiful to see this woman backstroke, slide under the waves, reemerge in the undertow. Then she's back at her clothes, shaking water from her hair. "Felicity," she tells me, before we part. "But everyone calls me Fliss."

"STOP!" CALLS A SKINNY GUY in a red kayak as he speed paddles toward Melissa and me. "Stay *away* from the edge."

He bumps his kayak against Melissa's. It's our second warning. "If I have to tell you again, it's no more kayaking."

Kayaking is only "free" on Pier 38 in the monetary sense. We're contained in a tightly prescribed square. I understand why. The Kayaking Club takes the space it's given, and the club's volunteers are sensitive to losing their permit after a guy recently broke bad and paddled straight across the Hudson to New Jersey.

We promise to be more careful, and he paddles away. We'd drifted because we'd been in a heavy discussion. After the wilderness trip — and particularly after the day at Rockaway and meeting Fliss — I'd been feeling walled-in. The usual urban sanctuaries were failing to provide the kind of mind-body balance I deeply needed. I'd been trying to convey this, but Melissa didn't get me. Then she began talking about "turf war and power grab" at her office. I didn't get her.

After the patrol kayak leaves us alone again, we paddle away from square's edge, toward "our" royal blue sailboat. We are both still really worked up. "I don't know," Melissa says. "I guess part of me's jealous that you idle in the mountains and at the beach while I'm in glass towers."

I plunge my paddle deep, feeling frustrated. "Slow doesn't mean easy. It's not like I'm a…a fluffy guinea pig in a bed of *Daily News* shreddings, blissfully chomping celery all day." Even as I say this, I realize it makes no sense. "Slow is…*feeling* the changes in weather, a kind of gnawing itch in the back of my throat. More possum than guinea pig."

"I'm not getting you," Melissa says, as we moor on the sailboat. I don't even get myself. Beyond Industrial Time, language slips, and I'm caught on something Fliss mentioned to me before we parted. She spoke about "going feral" by following nature's rules, not civilization's. *Feral*. The word makes me shudder a little; I'm afraid of wanting it.

We bob beside our sailboat. We aren't daydreaming today. The adjacent pier's concrete, military-controlled power station blocks most of Lady Liberty. I can just see her torch punching through and Jersey City's wall of modernist buildings. Melissa and I have been reading a book together called *Mating in Captivity*. A good friend in Rhode Island recommended it to us as we grapple with a new marriage and the prospect of having kids. The book's author, New York City psychotherapist Ester Perel, explains that most animals lose interest in mating when they're caged. She advises couples to escape the domestication boxes that disconnect them from the inner wildness that constitutes people's base nature. It's a wildness that is available in the city or in nature — because it's what we are — and it's the key to successful coupledom.

"Do we want to raise a child in a box?" I ask.

Melissa is silent. I know how much she longs for a child. I do, too. I love Melissa and want to share with her the very real and natural experience of giving birth and creating a family. For me there's hardly anything more primal — *feral* — than doing what creatures do: reproduce, raise young. I am aware of the overpopulation crisis, and of how it fuels the environmental crisis, and I deeply respect those who choose, for whatever combination of reasons, to refrain from reproducing. However, in our conversations, Melissa and I have talked about how, by raising a child with love and ecological values, one arguably does the planet, and others, a service. But is it possible to foster such values in a modern city?

And there's another dimension to it for me. I am a parent already, and nothing in my life has compared to the birth of my daughter, Amaya, and the love I feel for her every day. We're synched, Amaya and me, feeling through the same heart. I wonder how to accommodate a blended, dispersed family. Having a child with Melissa would not supplant the love I have for

Amaya, but it would be a second chance at creating a family, *a whole* that would include Amaya.

We're drifting again toward square's edge, both of us lost in thought. *If we do this,* I think, *I'd have a child beside me every day, not just on summer vacations.* All the times I've had to say good-bye to Amaya before she goes back to her mom. I wouldn't have to say good-bye.

"Oh shit," Melissa says. Mr. Red Kayak is bee-lining our way. Tripped the wire again.

I RETURN TO ROCKAWAY the next day, but no Fliss.

I haven't brought any work. I haven't brought any ideas about how the day, a Thursday, should go, except that a side of me — maybe a feral one — wants to reconnect with Fliss. I'm blue about the tiff with Melissa and conflicted about just about everything. So I walk. Walk barefoot for miles as waves crash. Having packed food and water, I make it through Fort Tilden and all the way to Breezy Point. The farther I trod, the fewer the tool-bearers, and by Breezy, MM's voice lessens to a hush.

My toe pads wrinkle from the hours walking the surf. After lunch, a pod of four dolphins swims by, off-shore. I parallel the pod, until the dolphins dive below and don't resurface. The water speaks to me. "Language," writes French philosopher Maurice Merleau-Ponty, "is the very voice of the trees, the waves, and the forests." Walking the tide line I think of how words like "splash," "gush," and "wash" flow out of the sounds water makes and through our vocal cords. Water helps create the Natural City for me, not just through its calming presence, but also by inhabiting me through the words I utter. David Abram expresses it like this in *The Spell of the Sensuous*:

We regularly talk of howling winds, and of chattering brooks. Yet these are more than mere metaphors. Our own languages are continually nourished by these other voices — by the roar of waterfalls and the thrumming of crickets.... If language is not a purely mental phenomenon but a sensuous, bodily activity born of carnal reciprocity and participation, then our discourse has surely been influenced by many gestures, sounds, and rhythms besides those of our single species.

The moon rises just before sunset. Melissa has texted that she has to attend a cocktail party with her boss, so I decide to catch the moonrise from a lifeguard chair. A side of me is tempted to grab a twenty-four-ounce — or three of them — from a 116th Street grocer, but instead, I will myself to meditate. As the sun snuffs out and the sky goes black under a bleached moon, I repeat the *Sat Nam* mantra Melissa and I have chanted so many times with Amanbir. *Sat Nam*: My path is truth.

The first glimpse I get of Fliss is her teeth and eyes, white in the moonlight. I stand up in the lifeguard chair. She's out there, swimming in the waves! I watch Fliss until she comes ashore fifty yards west and heads in the opposite direction. Through the sand, I jog toward her. When I reach her she smiles.

"Watch my stuff a sec?" I say.

The water is cold on my chest. I dive under a wave and swim against the current. Sharks and stingrays stalk below, and I'm a little fearful of the dark unknown, but I want to catch a moonlit wave. Bobbing in the darkness, I wait.

The waves are small at first, but then a big set begins. "Never take the first wave" is a body-surfing principle I learned in Liberia. I let the first big one bury me, then resurface with a gasp. There's no Natural City here — just splash, gush, and thunder. Seeing my wave, I breaststroke furiously shoreward. Just before I'm taken — an instant straining time — I'm suspended between my will and the ocean's, citizen and rebel, captive and feral.

7. THE PHYSICS OF HAPPINESS

"CONGRATULATIONS," THE EMAIL READS. "We're pleased to offer you a position teaching 'Sustainable Development' to New York University Master's students of international affairs."

The message seems foreign. I reread it, and only then remember that I applied for the position some months back. They want me. They want me to start right away. Start... a *job*.

It's as if the Cornelia Street crack dealer has come along and tempted me with the potent, familiar drug of work.

Just say no, I tell myself, walking through a Washington Square Park that now looks different. I brush past William the Pigeon Guy and feathery Chico — I'm hypnotized by the grandiose-purple NYU flags flying over half the buildings on the square. I hardly hear Bruce and the Jam as I aim for NYU's towering Bobst Library on Washington Square South. I step into its grandeur. The twelve-story library makes miniscule the tiny idlers in the park below.

"ID, please," says the security guard.

I tell him I don't have one.

"Sorry, NYU ID holders only."

With a faculty ID, I could access two million items in the Bobst Collection, work out at the NYU gym, and utilize dozens more university facilities throughout the city. I could influence nascent minds. And earn money.

"I don't know," I tell Melissa, at the end of Pier 45 that evening. There's a rainbow over the Hudson, but I'm only half-seeing it.

"Seems like a no-brainer to me," she says. "It's just one class."

"For now, yes. But that's still three hours a week in the classroom plus triple that in prep time. Designing the class from scratch, grading papers, faculty meetings..." Just thinking about it takes me out of the Slow Year's pulse. Not only would I be stepping toward the workaholic precipice, but it would require a costume change. Professor Powers can't idle on the dock of the bay, wasting time in a pair of cutoffs. What if the dean saw him?

THE NEXT DAY, I'm some fifty miles up the Hudson from Pier 45, skinny-dipping in the Doodletown Reservoir in Bear Mountain State Park. A countercyclical, hour-and-a-quarter Shortline bus ride to paradise. The buses coming into the city were packed, but I was one of just three people riding it *up* the Hudson. It's a Wednesday, normally the second and last day of my workweek, but inspired by the Adirondacks camping trip, I decide August should be a month of seven-day weekends. Remember summer?

I float, the breeze rippling across the pond, then dive into the cool depths and resurface. The mossy banks and rippling jack pines seem as delighted as I am. Thoughts of any job are a galaxy away.

I sunbathe, feeling like the only soul in the fifty-two-thousand-acre park complex. Later, a little reluctantly, I dress and hike the ghost town that is Doodletown. Once a bustling village, Doodletown slowly dwindled in population as the local mining business dwindled. In the 1960s, Bear Mountain State Park bought out the final residents and let the park swallow the town. Or nearly so. The foundations for a hundred homes, the schoolhouse, and the general store remain along partly grown-over streets. The progeny of pear, apple, and peach trees freckle the forest. I half expect a Doodletown resident to emerge from one of the overgrown groves.

Leaving Doodletown, I hike seven miles through the Catskill hills. I achieve one expansive view of the Hudson, but trails are mostly walled by high forest. As night falls, I return to my room on the third floor of Bear Mountain Lodge, a hundred-year-old building inside the park. I'm one of but a few midweek guests. Rates are half of what they are on weekends — another countercyclical bonus. I sleep by my window, Hessian Lake below, and dream of a thriving Doodletown, before it was erased like a doodle in the margin. In the morning I rise early and climb a dewy trail far above Doodletown, along a stretch of the 2,180-mile Appalachian Trail to the peak of Bear Mountain. Sweating, I reach the summit, and — all alone — look down over ridges of forested hills and the curves of the Hudson.

Something prickly like the spikes of a cactus lies way out

past the farms that break up the forest beyond Bear Mountain and Harriman State Park. The day is clear blue, there's the ribbon of the Hudson, and could that be...the New York City skyline?

Though I'm at a hard northern angle, that skinny spike is the Empire, the Chrysler to its left, the Bank of America to the right. A moment ago I felt isolated in the wilderness; now I'm visually linked to the ripple-city. There's the Bronx blurring into Midtown, and closer still, Yonkers. Westchester County lies directly across the river.

At the peak of Bear Mountain, I'm in a city stretching along the Hudson, from Pier 45 in the Village to the riverbank just below me. Even as I start my familiar utopian daydream — this time, John de Graaf, US Secretary of Labor, enacts three-day workweeks, and the Shortline buses and new light-rail trains are equally full both ways — a sudden, monstrously loud, and completely unanticipated noise blows apart my musings.

A fire truck? No, it's a good ten times the volume of any I've ever heard. Unable to think, I scamper down an embankment to the Appalachian Trail and follow it toward Bear Mountain Inn and Hessian Lake.

As I jog downward, the sound only grows. It's an alarm of the most shocking proportions. A flock of Canada geese takes flight to escape the noise, and I pin a finger deep into each ear. Amazingly, this does little to mute it.

Then I come upon a towering megaphone half-concealed in trees. I'm descending not just through a forest but through a forest of warnings, and it strikes me that this shrill sound could only be one thing — a big, dangerous something on the east side of the Hudson just across from Bear Mountain State Park. Till now, I've ignored it, but the Indian Point nuclear power plant now has my full attention.

All of a sudden, the sound stops. A robotic voice echoes through the trees. "This was a test," the cyborg says. "In the case of an actual emergency, this alarm would be followed by evacuation instructions..."

I arrive at a ridge overlook and see the nuclear facility, a sprawling industrial complex on the Hudson's east bank. It's of the same design as the Fukushima nuclear power plant that melted down in Japan after a 2011 earthquake, displacing fifty thousand households after radiation leaked into the air, soil, and sea, leading to bans on shipments of fish and vegetables. Cars on Highway 202 rush by Indian Point toward, a stone's throw to the north, the West Point military base and academy.

Later that day, at dusk, I return to Doodletown.

It doesn't look quaint anymore. Evacuated homes, an irradiated reservoir, the Bronx and Yonkers quarantined, and the Hudson life-free. A military jet from West Point slices to the east, and I think of something *New York Times* columnist Thomas Friedman wrote: "McDonald's cannot flourish without McDonnell Douglas....The hidden fist that keeps the world safe for Silicon Valley's technologies to flourish is called the US Army, Air Force, Navy, and Marine Corps."

Nuclear Indian Point–powered, West Point–defended Manhattan. Its mega-banks capitalize America's 956 international military bases and provide billions for our nuclear and — yes — "defensive" biological and chemical weapons. Little is more invisible than the things I want to ignore, and each Slow

Day I will such facts into invisibility. Only the shrill alarm wakes me up. Now I see, in a dark Doodletown, something like suicide.

"OH, THE ABSOLUTELY WORST THING HAS HAPPENED!" reads the email from Tim, a good friend of Melissa's and mine. "My son took his life on Wednesday."

Reading this, I reel. Melissa had just written Tim a cheery email, and this is the response.

Tim's son, Dwight, was twenty-five. I'd never met him, but I knew he served in the US Marines in Afghanistan. He had not been all right since returning from the war eight months back. Dwight had been sleeping on the sofa each night in front of the TV, his pistol under the pillow. The same gun he used on himself.

Later, as I sit cross-legged on Tar Beach beside my old friend from college, Brock, this news is on my mind — the email blaring like the Bear Mountain alarm — and I share it. After, we gaze south in silence toward Wall Street and the Freedom Tower. The branches of our tree scrape on brick, and its leaves cast patchy shadows over us.

"Roofs threaten," Brock finally says. "That's why you and Melissa are the only ones who ever come up here. Most people are probably afraid they might jump."

Brock has a handsome nose, wavy dark brown hair — receding a bit — and crisp green eyes. He's a beautiful man, a mix of his fair-skinned Massachusetts dad and striking Iranian mom. He continues: "When I look into the branches of that tree, I'm half-scared I might jump into them, to swing and climb."

(margin note: suicide of friend's son)

I remember another friend, Susan, who stood up here with me when we first moved in. Her face held a look similar to Brock's now. Flushed of cheek, gleaming of eye, slightly wild. Susan, on the cusp of middle age, and with two gorgeous young children and an amazing husband and everything fabulous, said, "I don't want to get too close to the edge. I don't trust that part of me that could just for no particular reason... *leap*."

I know what Brock and Susan mean. Tar Beach is exquisitely tainted. Five seconds away is death, a freefall of about a floor per second. Death's a visceral companion that counterintuitively props *up* my spirits, generates the roof's gravity. When death is five seconds away, what matters telescopes into the millisecond of now, and I feel lighter, more present.

"I use my office-building roof for naps," Brock says. "I sneak up there every day for a half hour, set my phone alarm, and sleep! March through November, at least. I bundle when it's cooler, and there's an awning for rain. When snow and ice cover the roof, I nap on the carpeted stairwell-top. Nobody's ever nabbed me. Five hundred others in the building and no one seeks the roof."

"The siesta is under attack all over the world," I say. The sun arches over the stairwell portal — 3 PM — leaving us in the shade, the downtown view now blazing Technicolor. "Naps interfere with global competitiveness, say the critics." The Bolivian Congress eliminated the two-hour lunch break *con siesta* for all public employees. The private sector did, too. "Urban Bolivians used to have a refreshing thirty-minute nap after a long lingering lunch with family. Now they scarf down a burger at their desk."

"I *have* to take a nap," Brock says, standing up to stretch, "or I can't work in the afternoon. Body refuses."

"Research shows that a nap actually increases productivity at work because of the recharge."

"But it's soft. Like the kindergarten nap. Workaholics hate it."

"It's the ultimate in nondoing," I say, "like the yoga pose *savasana*: the corpse."

Brock walks over to the edge, reaches up and touches a leaf on one of the branches. Watching him, I feel a touch of vertigo. I remember when I first met him, in a class we shared sophomore year. On the first day, the professor had us do a mock international negotiation simulation, and Brock represented China. He floored everyone, delivering a confident *realpolitik* lambasting of the rest of us. *Brilliant bullshitter*, I thought, and I immediately admired and slightly envied his Neal Cassady looks and pluck. We became quick friends. We were just shy of twenty years old.

Now we're twice that. Brock's lost in thought, his profile against the Freedom Tower. There's a looser quality to the skin on his face and his neck, a bit more breadth around the waist, the chest, the arms. But not much. He's still cool, and young enough, and women continue to chase him. Still, he's changed since last year, when he almost died. Drunken rowdies, out of nowhere, pummeled Brock on a Midtown Friday night, and he spent months in the hospital with a severe concussion. The experience didn't cynically steel him, but now that he's healed, he seems deeper somehow.

I take the twelve steps down to our micro and return to Tar Beach with two mugs of coffee, handing one to Brock, who immediately starts talking about fishing. Since recovering from the concussion, he's been rising at 4 AM many workdays to fish for striped bass in the Hudson. "Powers, remember that full-moon night on Long Island? When those striped bass practically jumped onto the dock for us?"

I nod. Of course, I remember. We were twenty-three, just after college. Those huge fish gleamed in the moonlight as we hauled them in, rods doubled with the weight. We threw most back, but saved two to grill up with lemon, and it tasted good. It's not the first time Brock's recounted this story to me. I realize that if prayer is a concentration of positive thoughts, so too can storytelling act as kundalini visualization. Striped bass gleaming in the moonlight, testing our muscles, nourishing our gullets, embodying our friendship. His story rejuvenates.

Just before he leaves — to "shoot stick" with a buddy at an East Harlem pool hall — I tell him about Fliss, how she talked about getting "feral."

"*Feral?*" He smiles. "I'd love to meet this Fliss."

I tell him I can probably arrange something.

"ARE YOU OKAY?" Melissa asks me. We're in our only-room, and I've just told her about my conversation with Brock, about Tar Beach, the five seconds, and Brock being afraid of jumping into the tree canopy.

Late August heat positively funnels up into our apartment, and our one mini-air-conditioner barely cuts through it. "I keep thinking about Dwight. The bloody scene in the bathroom when Tim found him. Found his son."

"*Honey*," she says, taking my hand.

Over a dinner of pasta, eaten Japanese-style on cushions

on the floor, we talk about kids. "Imagine having a child," I say, "and then finding him, one day, the way Tim did."

Melissa puts down her fork. "I'm thinking of that Galway Kinnell poem," she says. "Something about the courage it takes to give birth to a being that will someday die."

WHEN I BIKE TO OUR RENDEZVOUS POINT in the Ramble in Central Park, Fliss is already schooling Brock in the wild edibles found in Central Park. "I harvest cattail and chickweed," she tells him, "and the Kentucky coffee tree's pod makes amazing decaf. There's also sassafras here — used to make root beer."

They pause to greet me, but their eyes immediately lock back on each another. Fliss is as attractive in jeans and a tank top as she was in her one-piece on Rockaway Beach, her black hair pulled back haphazardly in a loose bun. Brock, playing hooky from his corporate job today, looks trim and gallant in his shorts and Ramones T-shirt. They've barely met, but I can already see sparks, and I feel a little proud of my matchmaking. It was my idea to have Fliss share her edible-plant knowledge with us.

However, as Fliss talks excitedly about Japanese knotweed and wild carrots, about the berries and American persimmons we'll seek, along with "gingko biloba, for refining memory," I can't quite muster my enthusiasm. I'm still feeling heavy-hearted about Dwight's suicide, and so I make an excuse and leave Brock and Fliss to themselves. They don't seem particularly upset.

I bike the full Central Park loop at top speed, then I pedal west on 116th and north to Sakura Park. Gravity brings me here. I dismount and look across the park down the street where the poet Rachel Wetzsteon used to live.

I only met Rachel once, three years back. We were both invited to speak at the Paterson College Writer's Conference in Wayne, New Jersey. The conference organizers arranged for the same car service to pick both of us up — first me in Queens, then her in Manhattan, one block from here. We connected instantly, sharing tidbits about our lives and writing. She'd published celebrated poems in the *New Yorker* and was a tenured English professor at Paterson. At the conference, we each signed a book to the other. On the way home, the forty-two-year-old Rachel was quiet, then she began crying. By the time we reached her apartment, she was sobbing on my shoulder. She'd broken up with her partner of several years, she told me. In the process, she'd lost the relationship she'd had with his children from a previous marriage. "I'd come to feel like a mom to them," she said amid tears, "and now they've been wrested from me."

The driver was patient. He waited, double-parked, as Rachel clasped my arm and spilled her story. I listened — nodding, trying to comfort her — but not knowing quite how to react. We'd just met that morning. Rachel Wetzsteon was a stranger. When she finally got out and we pulled away from the curb, the driver said to me: "That's New York for you. Ten million people and you're all alone."

A week later Rachel committed suicide.

For some time after, a part of me blamed myself. I could have asked for her phone number and checked in with her the next day. I could have let someone know. Eventually, the guilt drained out, replaced by a bag of gold coins.

I've carried it ever since. Every few months, I will find myself biking by Sakura Park or notice on my shelf the book of poems, entitled *Sakura Park*, she'd signed to me, and I'll touch the hundred shimmering moments of life I've been given since the last time I'd recalled Rachel. To me, each of them is a gold coin, and those coins — and not a savings account — are my wealth. When I run my hand through this bag of gold, I'm bewildered that Rachel cannot accumulate hers. In the poem entitled "Sakura Park," Rachel writes:

The park admits the wind,
the petals lift and scatter

like versions of myself I was on the verge
of becoming; and ten years on

and ten blocks down I still can't tell
whether this dispersal resembles

a fist unclenching or waving good-bye...

From Sakura Park, the Hudson gleams in cobalt lacquer. *Ten million people and you're all alone.* I call my daughter. She answers on the third ring.

"What are you doing?" Amaya asks.

I pause before answering. "I'm gazing over the world's most lovely river," I say.

Through the phone, I hear a cat meow. A Bolivian cat, four thousand miles south. "What are you doing?" I ask.

Amaya tells me she's playing with Blackie, Pinky Pie, Principe, and Princessa — her four kitty cats. She gave Pinky Pie warm milk for her first birthday yesterday. And she's watching mangoes ripen on her courtyard tree. "They're as big as empanadas now," she says.

After we hang up, I bike down to the river. The sun is setting, and I sneak down to some boulders below the bike path, take off my sandals, and slip my feet into the water. I miss Amaya, wish my child were closer to me. If Melissa and I conceive, another child will be. But that won't lessen the distance from Amaya.

"Hold the sadness and pain of *samsara* in your heart," says the Buddhist teacher Chögyam Trungpa Rinpoche, as told by Pema Chödron. "And at the same time the power and vision of the Great Eastern Sun. Then the warrior can make a proper cup of tea." To me Slow Life, like meditation, is more than an escape from the daily grind. It's what's happening to me when I go off the drug of distraction. Sadness has the space to grow; *samsara*, or life's transience, its emptiness. My mind drifts to NYU, how taking that job could elbow out some of the pain. The Hudson flows south, to Amaya.

A FEW DAYS LATER, I'm in Washington Square Park, on the edge of the Jam. As Bruce solos a Neil Young tune, I'm writing questions in my Bolivian notebook, questions I could ask my "Sustainable Development" graduate students should I take the plunge. I've brainstormed exciting topics and readings — I can freely craft the course. I think of The 4-Hour Workweek, and how I could "double bill" by assigning the very readings I've been planning to do myself anyway. And how about a class that sprouts from my Slow practice of *caminando preguntando?* Gadflies in Manhattan.

Yesterday, after yoga, I asked Amanbir for advice on the job decision. We were sipping yogi tea in the Golden Bridge lounge downstairs. "There's a story I heard in India," he said. "It's about the proper stages in a person's life. There's a time to learn, up to age twenty-five. Then there's a time to do, up to age forty maybe." He sipped his tea. "And then there's a time to teach."

After that I called John de Graaf in Seattle. He also suggested I accept the job offer. "But for me work is like an addiction," I countered. "And what about 'Take Back Your Time'?"

De Graaf laughed. "Thomas Jefferson, man!" he said. "Not *all* of it."

I close my notebook, stuff it into a pocket, and wave to Bruce, who's tuning his guitar between songs. He nods back, and then I'm off. Off to the apartment to meet Melissa, who just texted she's home. I want to tell her the news: I've decided to take back my time, but not all of it. I'm going to teach.

My heart clicks fast as I cross the park. There's William with his pigeons, and when I reach him, Chico leaves from his shoulder and alights on mine. William hands me almonds, and I feed them to Chico, who swallows them whole. The bird's weight on my shoulder, I think of the "Physics of Happiness," which I discovered, some years back, tacked to the wall of the 12 x 12 cabin in North Carolina and attributed to Albert Camus:

Life in the open air.
Love for another being.
Freedom from ambition.
Creation.

Only those four. I give Chico my last almond — what could be freer from ambition? Chico flaps back to William, and I cross Sixth Avenue, pass Papaya Dog, thread the horse entrance, and climb the Cornelia stairs two at a time.

Melissa's not in the apartment.

I find her on Tar Beach, under the tree, standing at roof's edge.

Too close. Five seconds too close. Melissa pivots and steps. Away from the edge. Toward me. Her smile rises into summer's-end green, the fertile halo of our tree canopy above. Her light-green eyes pick up the setting sun, and the first leaves of autumn wink in red and dirty blonde. I'll tell her about Sakura Park and *samsara*. I'll tell her I'm going to teach.

Melissa hugs me, firmer and longer than she has in a while. Over her shoulder, on the fire escape where the baby doves used to live, one of the largest spider webs I've ever seen snatches the sun's rust. The hug times out, and Melissa looks into my eyes. "I'm pregnant," she says.

A leaf detaches from a branch above us and somersaults down, down, down. Five stories down, to land safely. We smile and whisper, two mammals on a ledge. A pigeon flock races overhead, flaring south toward the Freedom Tower's lights, along the Hudson's flow.

PART 2

AUTUMN
Frankenstorm

8. CONSUMED

AUTUMN COMES EARLY TO GREENWICH VILLAGE. Chilly northern winds blow down the Hudson, and all New York is in flux. Migrating birds cross New York Harbor, from the Rockaways to Staten Island. Washington Square Park's sunflowers sag their heavy heads toward the ground more each day; somebody lops them off for the seeds just before I arrive to harvest one or two heads myself. The Jam meets less frequently, and the park's classical pianist slips into autumn-evoking Mahler pieces. Amanbir leaves for India to visit the Golden Temple in Amritsar. Beautiful monarch butterflies flutter through Central Park, past the growing Freedom Tower, and even over the Brooklyn Bridge as they migrate three thousand miles to overwintering grounds in Mexico. On Fifth Avenue one nippy day, I stop to gaze. Just above the heads of pedestrians, hundreds of them wing south to Mexico, their ephemeral reflections on the Tiffany storefront.

And the bluefish run early. One day, a Chinese fisherman hoists a fifteen-pound blue up onto Pier 45, its silvery body suddenly flapping violently on the Greenwich Village pier. Fifty people gather around, snapping photos of this sudden intrusion into the city of the fall fish run.

NYU students flood back into Washington Square Park after their summer break, and I find myself selecting readings, designing lesson plans, and — a little nervously — meeting my Sustainable Development students for the first time. To set up a practical class for my students, I ride the R to Brooklyn Grange. Up on the rooftop farm, I find Anastasia, her hands covered in soil. She agrees to host my students, then quickly rejoins a cluster of squash pickers. It's harvest time, and the change is enormous from my early-season visit. Now the roof is lush with ten-foot trellised tomatoes, abundant zucchini, and sagging sunflowers ringing nearly the entire acre, their yellow faces winking down into the traffic.

class
field trip

"I think I hear something," I say, one morning on Tar Beach, my ear to Melissa's belly.

She tousles my hair. "Not yet."

But "belly-baby" — as we come to call the miracle inside Melissa — becomes audible to us during the doctor's visit, where we hear the pinhead heartbeat for the first time and see a grainy sonogram image. I stop drinking alcohol along with Melissa in a kind of "ghost pregnancy," and we begin a forty-day couple's meditation. Each evening, we sit cross-legged, our backs firmly together, and sing a mantra as belly-baby slowly grows.

One day, a greeting card arrives. A relative, enthusiastic about the pregnancy, mails us a "Congratulations!" Hallmark card. As I open it, a plastic gift card slides out, worth $75 at the chain store Buy Buy Baby.

It's well intentioned, but the thought of inhabiting the box "parent consumer" makes me squeamish. Nor do I want belly-baby — still in the womb — implicitly encouraged to buy *buy*.

I'm frustrated for an hour or so, but then I have an idea.

"I'M SORRY, BUT I CAN'T ISSUE A CASH REFUND," our local Buy Buy Baby manager says, handing the $75 gift card back to me.

"But our child is still a bean sprout," I say.

"You'll need us soon enough." He smiles. "It doesn't expire. And you can refill it. It's like a debit card."

"But the $75 will be a donation to Campaign for a Commercial-Free Childhood. They do great work."

"I wish I could help."

"You can. Do you know that Greece bans all television ads for toys between 7 AM and 10 PM?"

"Is that so?"

I nod. "And advertising to children under twelve is banned in Norway and Sweden. That way their tots don't have to view 200,000 commercial messages during their brain-tender years, like ours do."

The manager is no longer smiling. To my left squawks an incessant Sweet Talkin' Puss in Boots ("Give me your hands, baby," the toy metallically intones, "they're so soft!"). Advertising operates on the principle of repetition. Children, like grown-ups, are more likely to desire an object if they hear the message several times. Psychologist Tim Kasser of Knox College is one of the many researchers who argues for a ban on childhood advertising, and he urges parents to "limit exposure to materialistic messages," such as television and commercials.

"Buy Buy Baby?" I say, still dumbfounded by the name. "Is that supposed to be ironic?"

"It's the name of the store, *sir*." His arms are stiffly akimbo. I've outworn my welcome. I realize I should be berating the company's CEO, if anyone, not a retail store manager who's hardly responsible for our consumer society.

When I leave, I'm still holding the plastic card.

"We need a policy," I say to Melissa that evening, back at the micro. "A Borrow Borrow Baby policy. Everything for belly-baby...second-hand."

Melissa doesn't reply. She looks at our sole painting, her Fafa's winter landscape above our bed. "I agree," she says, though it's obvious she doesn't, not completely. "But how do you tell people, diplomatically, not to give baby gifts?"

She lies next to me on the bed. I slip my hand under her shirt, onto her belly. "We say they can show their love by donating to Squeaker's education fund."

"Or how about to an education fund for needy children?" Melissa suggests.

We talk about *The Story of Stuff*— Annie Leonard's excellent twenty-minute documentary, which so vividly unravels consumerism — and how each *new* plastic toy and diaper means more carbon belched into the atmosphere in order to create it. We decide to sift through the various "minimalist parenting" Internet sites and create a simplicity kit of baby items and then stock it with second-hand items from friends and siblings.

The conversation surfaces a larger issue when Melissa says: "It's interesting how we've been trying to create a culture-within-the-culture for our twosome. But when we're three, there'll be a totally new culture to make."

I gaze out the window. A good third of our tree's leaves have changed to rust, orange, and brown. "How about...a kind of True North for our family?"

"Exactly. Not the Magnetic North of consumerism you get slurped into when you have kids."

This excites us. We've made so much progress, over several months, developing Urban Slow practices of simplicity, spirituality, and leisure. Now we can adapt the ideas to family life. We make a plan: we'll take a couple of hours with poster paper and markers and imagine our True North vision for family.

We set a date. One week away.

Meanwhile, I find myself especially sensitive to what's going on in the lives of the New York City parents around me. I watch a young mom in Madison Square Park hand her whining two-year-old an iPhone with a bubble-blowing app. It calms the child, who blows on the screen, creating electronic bubbles that float into a digital sky.

Melissa and I have dinner with a Turkish-American friend

preschool admission

from graduate school, Ahmed — an investment banker — and his wife, Malinka. They talk, in stressed tones, about nursery schools for their three-year-old. "I've applied to nine," Malinka laments, "but eight rejections so far. You have to have an in. It's like a mafia of the rich." She talks about hiring a "preschool admissions coach" at $250 an hour.

Melissa asks her why getting into an elite nursery school is so important. Ahmed shakes his head. "If you don't go to Malvern or Columbus Park West, forget about a good elementary school."

I raise an eyebrow. He laughs. "You're too granola to get this, Powers. Mediocre elementary school equals mediocre high school equals mediocre college."

Many equal signs, little equality. Ahmed and Malinka are fighting to pay up to $40,000 a year for preschool ("plus mandatory 'donations' on top of that," Ahmed adds) for the exposure to bluer blood. Your kids befriend theirs, and you nudge into society. Welcome to the One Percent. The high price tag is also due to plain old supply and demand — a ratcheting up on the most competitive island on Earth.

AS I STRUGGLE TO SQUARE BELLY-BABY with New York City, something a little eerie happens on the subway one afternoon.

I'm on the A train, heading to Central Park, when I overhear something that snaps me out of the mantra I'm repeating in my head. "Holy shit, dude, that game's *wicked* fresh!"

I look up to see a twenty-something hipster in baggy pants, fashionably tousled hair, and what looks to my untrained eye as the very latest Nikes.

"Never played one this rad," replies another guy, equally cool. "What's it called?"

"Clean Up."

"Clean Up?"

"Yeah. It's just like $10 or something in the App Store."

"I'm scoring that!"

"Yeah... Clean the freak *up!*"

During this exchange, I notice many of our fellow riders tuning in to this animated exchange. When people experience someone getting excited about something, we become curious, and we mirror their excitement. Brain scientists call this phenomenon "neural mirroring." All the more so, it would seem, when one is eavesdropping and serendipitously hearing about the Next Awesome Thing.

I'm a little curious about the game myself, but something smells a little off about the exchange. I had recently happened upon a magazine article about something called "stealth advertising," a kind of commercialization of the space of overhearing. Companies pay actors to name drop their brand in parks and on sidewalks.

The train pulls up at the 14th Street station. I watch the two hipsters get up, say "later" to one another, then exit. I get up to look out the door. The hipsters don't exit to the street, but rather reenter the next subway car through separate doors!

Going into private-eye mode, I leave the car and follow the hipsters. Unnoticed by them, I sit down several seats away from where the pair has reseated themselves.

"Stand clear of the closing doors." The doors shut, and the train rumbles north. My heart clicks; I'm spying. For thirty seemingly endless seconds, the guys are quiet, one of them thumbing his smarty.

"Holy shit, dude, that game's *wicked* fresh!"

"Never played one this rad."

I'm paralyzed by a *Groundhog Day* feeling. Reality hits the repeat button.

"What's it called?"

"Clean Up."

Exactly as before, some dozen folks tune in, their brains mirroring the excitement. My mind computes: two minutes between stops, thirty play-acted conversations an hour, an average of a dozen people overhearing it. That's three hundred trend-setting New Yorkers, every hour, hearing from a seemingly impartial source about a hot new product.

I rise, displeased. Holding the hand railing as the train jolts forward, I walk in their direction, my indignity mixing with anxiety.

"I'm scoring that! Clean Up, right?" one of them says.

"You sound so surprised," I interrupt. "Almost as if you didn't have the *same conversation* a couple minutes ago."

"Whatever," one says.

"Are you guys marketing?" I say, hearing my voice catch. I'm talking too loud. "You just did the same spiel in the car in front of us. I followed you here."

Everyone's eyes are on us now.

"You a stalker?" the other dude says.

I'm boiling now, but they're not. Why should they be? I just announced to everyone, in an unsteady voice, that I've been secretly following them. The train slows, stopping at West 23rd. "Plenty of *locos* in this town," one says. Then they say "later" to each other and exit.

I slump back down into a seat. "Stand clear of the closing doors." The train rolls on, everyone averting eye contact with me. Still worked up, I try to explain to the passenger next to me about stealth marketing, about what *really* just happened. But he, a fifty-something black man whose seems to have heard it all in his day, just nods, indulging my fantasy for a patient minute before going back to his *Daily News*.

In a haze, I come out of the subway in front of the Shops at Columbus Circle and walk beneath the CNN billboard clock into Central Park. The science fiction portion of David Mitchell's novel *Cloud Atlas* depicts a future where corporations completely dominate to the point that people and robots alike are unaware that their language and actions tick along to a consumerist plan. This certainly wasn't *Cloud Atlas*, but to the people on that car, marketing *was* reality, and I was crazy for inhabiting a world of noncommercialized human interaction previously known as reality.

ONE EVENING, while I'm picking up some kimchi at the Korean grocer's around the corner from our apartment, a pair of bar-hopping young women come in behind me. One of them approaches me and says: "Like that hat."

I touch the beret on my head. Chartreuse plaid. It's Melissa's, and I threw it on because it was the first thing at hand as I walked out.

"Thanks," I say, realizing the hat unintentionally endows me with metrosexual cred. She tells me about a similar hat she has and then asks, "By the way, do you like tea?"

I tell her I'm more of a coffee guy.

"Oh, but teeaaa," she says, stretching out the word, her eyes alight. "I work at David's Tea. It's new here on Bleecker."

"Great," I say.

"Hey, since I work there, I can get you a free tea anytime. We have a thousand varieties. I could tell by that hat that you'd like something different. Just drop my name if I'm not there, and you'll get your tea."

I'm beginning to get an uncomfortable feeling. She's obviously out with her friend, partying, so why is she pushing a tea habit on me?

"Do you want to come by tomorrow?"

I tell her I'll try. We chat for another minute about the Village bar scene, and then I leave the shop.

On the walk back home, it fully hits me that her offer was calculated. She was selling tea. And yet, at the same time, she really *did* seem authentically interested in the hat and in talking about local bars. She didn't fake a human connection, but she used it. Afterward, I realize I had sensed her awkwardness: she knew what she was doing and did it reluctantly.

Later, after some online research, I discover that this is a trend. Some companies pay their employees to nonchalantly offer samples or discounts at any time during ordinary social interactions. Employees are rewarded with "points" toward raises and promotions, and if less than, say, ten people come in and mention your name during a month, you can be demoted. The worker's "free time" — and the space of casual encounters — is thus co-opted by the marketplace.

Melissa and I realize our Slow City tools need sharpening. And that includes our "smart filters."

Smart-filtering is another practice — along with living at the third story, urban sanctuaries, savoring food, and coming into Natural Time — that has developed in our Slow Year. It arose from something Pablo Picasso once said: that he would not mind imprisonment in solitary confinement because he could spend years contentedly enjoying the light patterns made by tightening and loosening the muscles of his closed eyes. Okay, he's Picasso, and he gets to be weird like that, right? Nevertheless, Melissa and I find it useful to smart-filter the city's advertising on taxi tops, buses, phone booths, and the billboards that increasingly appear as giant digital screens. We simply squint our eyes a little and — *voila!* — said advertisement is transformed into a pleasant blur of shape and color.

Gracias, Picasso. Melissa and I have been smart-filtering all manner of marketing, allowing the impressionist color and form to delight before we glance away. I've gotten to the point where I see almost none of the city's commercial content. As an adaptation, I just allow, without even squinting, the color and letter shapes of an ad to be received as if out of the corner of my eye. When, occasionally, an ad's message breaks through the filter, it feels like a vaccine — a slight pinch that inoculates me against an outbreak of consumerism.

But the game's a-changing. Melissa and I can't smart-filter everything, including what we overhear and our "spontaneous" social interactions. Walking our neighborhood one late afternoon before our planned True North meeting, I notice the ubiquitous shopping bags carried by every third person, which act as mini-billboards. "Shoegasm" and "Banana Republic" perforate the abstract art I'm failing to make out of them. Even when I succeed, I begin to notice the brands jumping from people's clothing, the as-seen-on-TV hairstyles. I overhear somebody mention the address of "an amazing sample sale" and feel paranoid they're planting the idea. My vaccine falters.

I escape to Tar Beach.

I thread our horse entrance and rise five flights to our most cloistered sanctuary. Here it's just our tree's changing colors and the silence of courtyards created by taller neighboring buildings. I breathe, seeing neither ad nor the echo of one through a pedestrian. I hear the Pompeii Church clock tower dong five times — Melissa will be arriving for True North, our family culture powwow. A pair of migrating cardinals flutter in the tree branches, and I know that here, beyond branding, we can freely think outside the Xbox.

But when Melissa walks through the roof door in her beige work suit, she's holding something: a red-velvet Decadence cupcake.

Two-inch-high white frosting! Exquisitely sprinkled! A come-on for that identical dessert slipped through my filter from a shop window the other day, and I thought: *Whither the lowly cupcake?* Alas, if humble salt and hamburgers can be exalted, why shouldn't the cupcake — that unassuming snack my mom used to pull from the oven for the neighborhood kids and me — also find within itself a subtler mouthfeel, a puffier icing, and most importantly of all, a pricier tag.

"How much?" I ask, nodding toward the cupcake.

"How much," Melissa repeats.

The cardinals dart off on a Midtown trajectory. Tar Beach is silent.

"How much was the cupcake?"

Melissa looks into the tree's colorful canopy, as if the answer might be up there. "Six-fifty?" It sounds like a question.

"Six...what? Dollars?"

"No, six Chinese yuan." She pulls poster paper and markers out of her briefcase. "Yes, dollars. It's a little treat, okay? Here. They're amazing. Take a bite."

"A one-dollar bite? I can't enjoy it knowing the bite costs a dollar." I rub my temples. I'm already stressed, and it's past the time of day when I usually drink java; I feel a caffeine headache coming on. "Have you seen the ads for that?"

"I thought you were smart-filtering the ads."

I mumble something about a clogged filter.

She fences her arms over her chest. "And anyway," she says, "you have your cappuccino splurges."

"*We* have *ours*. That's Slow ritual. This is the first six-fifty cupcake I've seen." I know I'm rationalizing. I was indoctrinated to want coffee until it became a biochemical need, just like every other Anglo-American — in fact, coffee is so central to our cultural identity it's chapter 1 in Christian Lander's satirical book *Stuff White People Like: A Definitive Guide to the Unique Taste of Millions*.

"Whoa! You're acting like I'm the only one on the roof who saw 200,000 ads a year. Last time I checked, your birth certificate didn't say Inuit."

Melissa and I stare at the immaculate cupcake. The comic irony skewers me as hard as my sudden migraine: two fully indoctrinated, embedded-in-the-matrix Americans think they can reengineer a family culture with a dozen felt-tipped pens? Our True North meeting has quickly gone south.

Our family vision session will have to wait, my lizard brain insists. We'll have it, eventually, but right now Melissa and I give in to indoctrination and head down the stairs to Prodigy for coffee accompanied by a red-velvet Decadence cupcake.

I CAN HAVE WHAT I WANT. But can I want what I want?

I write this on the whiteboard and look out into a seminar of ten twenty-somethings from five countries: my "Sustainable

Development" Master's students at NYU. It's our third class, and it feels a bit random to paraphrase Émile Durkheim like this and ask them to think about it. I notice a few of the students shifting uncomfortably in their seats.

Finally, one of the students, a twenty-four-year-old corn-fed Midwestern first-year named JT, says, "I don't get it. How could I not *want* what I want?"

I'm tempted to answer: cupcakes and Prodigy, stealth marketing and the death-of-spontaneous-interaction. Instead, I bite my tongue and allow silence to fill our small white classroom, tucked into a remote third-story corner of the historic 1913 Woolworth Building in the financial district.

Nicole, a fiery activist from San Francisco, raises her hand. "Well, Durkheim is the founder of sociology. So, if our desires are *socially* controlled, then maybe it's about whether or not we have *individual* freedom."

"Good," I say. "Can anyone give an example of that?"

"iPhones?" says another student, Bobby, from Guam. "Like how there's a newer, thinner one always coming out." He pulls an iPhone out of his pocket. "You feel self-conscious about having the old one. So, you buy the new one and then you *have* what you want. But because Apple's marketing — and peer-pressure — have shaped your desires, who knows what you would have *really* wanted in the first place!"

Found the smart kids. Half of the students are clueless about Durkheim's observation, but he and Nicole already nailed it.

"What does this have to do with 'sustainable development'?" asks one of the perplexed others.

"Excellent question," I say, and I write the 1987 United Nations Brundtland Commission's landmark definition of "sustainable development" on the board: *Development that meets the*

sustainable development

needs of the present without compromising the ability of future generations to meet their own needs.

I let that sit, then say: "If our conditioning into an all-pervading growth paradigm — a corporate-led globalization where the economy has to grow each year even though the ecosystem has limits — if that conditioning is so deep that we can no longer *want what we want*, maybe 'sustainable development' is magical thinking. Could civilization be headed for an inevitable, painful clash with the planet's biophysical limits?"

We debate the question, and clear camps emerge. Some students argue that technology will save the day: as environmental problems like climate change worsen, entrepreneurs will invent the needed green-tech fixes. Others insist that such market fixes kick in too late to avoid the "ecological tipping points" that trigger collapse.

I let the debate simmer and boil, then channel the group into the day's assigned reading — the writings of a brilliant contemporary anthropologist named Arturo Escobar.

Escobar's landmark 1994 book *Encountering Development* starts out by showing how "development" — bringing the "Third World" out of "poverty" — was *invented* and promulgated, after World War II, by the Western powers. Escobar then makes a fresh move. Our very vocabulary is so deeply colonized that, to be intellectually honest and indeed more scientific, we must step out of "development studies" as they are traditionally examined and view them as *discourse*: the embedded assumptions in the language itself must be unpacked and understood as supporting a certain worldview and political economy. "Development" is a linguistics we must view from the outside.

"I don't get Escobar," JT says, with appealing earnestness. "Poor countries need to develop just like us, right?" He runs a pen through his curly nut-brown hair.

"What's development?" I ask the class.

Bobby: "Economic, social, and cultural...progress?"

"What's development?" I ask again.

Nicole: "It's what 'developing' countries say it is. And I put that awful word in quotes because what are they developing *toward?* Us?!"

What's development?

We go around the circle. Ten students, ten different responses. Brain-scans suggests that questions activate several times more neural pathways than answers do. So, in the spirit of my Bolivian notebook, I ask. I ask about Escobar's complex ideas, ask them to consider Escobar through personal experience.

Slowly, a sense of openness fills our little white box tucked in the corner of Woolworth. One question begs another. *How can I begin to want what I want? Is the idea of progress invented or real? Are there alternatives to "growth"?*

"Professor?" JT raises his hand. "I'm confused."

A smattering of giggles. I repeat what Amanbir told me one day outside Golden Bridge: "If you're not confused, you're fused."

9. HIGH FIVE

NEW YORK INHALES, THEN EXHALES. West Side Highway traffic thunders, then fifty stoplights simultaneously wink to red, and pedestrians cross in the hush. Bleecker Street at midnight reeks of stale beer, then the sun rises to the scent of baguettes baking and fresh coffee at Amy's Bread. Melissa and I walk Manhattan's concrete, then head for the softer outskirts of the Natural City.

We start to wonder about another Natural City frontier, imagining the Rockaways as a minivacation. We ask around about lodging, but nobody has heard of a single hotel or B&B in the hardscrabble beach neighborhood. I finally do find one — and only one — online, the cheap and plain D. Piper Inn, which seems in keeping with Slow City adventure and thrift.

We ride a jostling A train through Brooklyn and Queens, stopping at aboveground stations with vibrantly colored vines climbing their platforms' barbed-wire fences — leaves flaming buttery yellow, chartreuse, pizza-sauce red. As we trundle over the Jamaica Bay wildlife reserve on a narrow bridge, Melissa spots thousands of Canada geese resting on the waters to the east, dark pointillist dots against the sapphire bay. A hundred dots disengage and morph into a honking flock that disappears over our train; our borough's just a little metallic patch in their southern migration.

Alighting at 116th Street, the last stop, Melissa and I are immediately approached by a drunk panhandler. Slurring, he asks for "a penny" — a clever bait-and-switch — smack in front of Rockaways Liquor. We walk a busy 116th Street lined with more liquor stores, Chinese food, and delis advertising COLD BEER and bustling with off-season surf bums and mentally handicapped people from the rehab centers lining the beach a block away. A short, middle-aged man — hardly much taller than he is wide — shakes his wooden cane at another, taller man, yelling for "the twenty bucks you owe me, fuck face!" Then he slaps the tall man on the back with his cane. "What's going on?" I ask a young guy passing me. He laughs and says: "The two of them do that routine every single day of the *week* on this corner."

Skirting interpersonal explosions, we drop down from the main boulevard and onto tranquil 114th Street, stopping in front of a ramshackle wooden house separated from the beach by several halfway houses and two hulking nursing homes. This is our home for the night: D. Piper Inn. It feels a bit ironic that within a subway ride of some of the most lavishly rich inhabitants of this little piece of Earth, it's the old, the sick, and the drug-addicted folks who get this prime view of the ocean. In the end they are the ones who could use the calm in their everyday, while the more ably fit choose to stay locked up in their glass towers a good distance from the beach. Rockaway seems to turn everything on its head and offer the deliciously unexpected.

Puppies greet us lavishly at the front door, their little tongues licking our fingers. Melissa picks up a pair; they squirm and nestle into her breasts, as if to nurse. She laughs, her pregnant belly, now more obvious, shaking slightly. The puppies' parents, shiny-smooth Cavalier King Charles spaniels, look on from the corner of the threadbare, musty lobby, disinterested. But they leap to their paws when their owner, D. Piper manager Peter — a gruff, fifty-something Irishman — barrels in. Peter leads us up three creaking sets of stairs to our room, boasting nonstop about the view and claiming we're "lucky it's off-season because D. Piper is booked solid through summer" and how we'd "normally never get this ocean-view room." Our single sea-facing window looks down a tunnel of similarly ramshackle homes and concrete buildings into a sliver of Atlantic Ocean. Reflexively, I scan for dolphins, for whales. Melissa spots a cruise ship coming out of New York Harbor.

We hang out in our little room. We beachcomb. Fliss is nowhere to be seen, the boardwalk restaurants and Blue Bottle Coffee are shut, and the lifeguards in their orange bathing suits are gone till next spring. Rockaway, on this nippy fall day, is beautifully forgotten. On the vacant beach, I strip down to my boxers and run into the freezing waves. I ride an icy one to shore. Melissa jogs over with a towel and wraps it around my chest, hugging it into me.

The next morning, we wake up late. Melissa leaves, coming back after a while with everything bagels, and we smear scallion cream cheese on them and chew in silence, our four feet mingling on the narrow windowsill. We gaze past our toes at our slice of Atlantic, and all at once, I'm suffused with an unexpected, prickly sorrow.

I awoke some twenty times the previous night beside Melissa in our narrow full-sized bed — "No queens?" I'd asked Peter on the phone when reserving. "*Full*," he asserted. "It's always worked." — and each awakening was a blessing. The sound of Melissa's breathing, the crash of distant waves. Twenty times I spooned into her, into our child-to-be. Asleep means unconscious. Awake means I feel Melissa's warmth, accumulate more gold coins of presence.

Now I'm blindsided by the fact that I'll die on a Wednesday or a Friday. Or on one of the other five days of the week. I won't wake up one morning, or I won't go to sleep one night. Melissa and I have one day left awake together or 11,098 or some other finite quantity. And so, as we walk the boardwalk after breakfast, seagulls slicing an irritated path through the slate gray sky, the air too thick with salt, I fight against this feeling. I want yesterday's joy to come back: our A train sailing across Jamaica Bay, ecstatic puppies, and the glowing, open ocean. But that joy's worn out, and what's left of it is sorrow. I can't bring myself to hold Melissa's hand.

A FEW DAYS LATER, I find out something new about my wife. We're at the Rock, a rock climbing gym in Astoria — on a three-day free trial — and she suddenly vanishes.

I bend down for a moment to tie a shoelace, and when I come back up her green eyes and dirty blonde hair are gone. I look to the blank climbing wall freckled with colorful, irregularly shaped handholds. I glance right. Left. Backward.

No Melissa in this enclosed universe of clanking iron free-weights, muted hip-hop from a Body Attack class in a side room, and the grunts of ripped-muscle climbers scaling impossibly vertical walls.

My eyes scan the climbers until one jumps out from the rest. It's a woman nearing the top carabiner. Strong shoulders; dirty blonde hair. A small tummy bump on her otherwise lithe figure. My wife.

· An instant later Melissa touches the top. As she freefalls back down on her ropes, she flashes me a satisfying smile with a hint of pleasure in knowing she surprised me. I know she used to mountaineer in the Bolivian Andes — she even climbed the 19,970-foot Huayna Potosí — but she was holding out on me about her rock-climbing prowess.

This free, three-day climbing vacation in the city — like our low-budget Rockaway weekend — is part of an experiment inspired by Vicki Robin and Joe Dominguez's *Your Money or Your Life*, which Melissa has been rereading. In pricey Manhattan, we've been exceeding our Slow Year's monthly budget, so we begin to explore what's free in New York. Melissa subscribes us to a daily email service called the Skint. Each day, it details dozens of "free and cheap" things to do in the city. Besides free Juilliard School recitals — and rock-climbing promotions — we discover Sundays at Lincoln Center: complimentary classical music in the music library auditorium. One Sunday, we bike the Hudson River path to Lincoln Center and lose ourselves in an hour and a half of Stravinsky and Bach, then bike Central Park. The day's expenses? Zero. And then there are the no-cost days at most of the city's museums (New Museum on Thursday; MoMA on Friday; Guggenheim on Saturday).

"Check this out," Melissa says one evening, handing me a leaflet she picked up. A free week at YogaWorks. Times four, actually. They have four Manhattan locations, and the unabashed cheapskate can snatch a week at each. Surfing around a bit, I realize that many of New York's two hundred yoga studios offer a similar promotion. That's four *years* of free yoga.

Am I chagrined at taking a free week of yoga that I have little intention of extending? Yes. Does my guilt stop me from joining YogaWorks? No. To not take the offer, I tell myself, feels akin to letting ripe mangoes rot on the tree. Melissa and I eat the mangoes.

YogaWorks, we discover, is completely different from humble Golden Bridge. The up-to-date, high-ceiling studio is a kind of spa-*cum*-lotus-pose, offering hot showers and fluffy towels, body creams and herbal teas, and computer terminals for quick karmic Tweets. All of it, free. YogaWorks. Yoga *must* work — the sleek-and-trim bodies breezing through the place prove it. Desk attendants, instructors, and even the marketing specialist who welcomes us and signs us up radiate full-moon-in-Tulum calm, decked out in the newest yoga trappings. Alas, there are incongruities. After one class, surprised by the mere one-minute corpse pose at the end of class, I'm told by the instructor: "If I do *savasana* for more than that, people start leaving. Too eager to get back to their iPhones, I guess." If only the original yogis back in India could see this scene. Hybrid yoga, adapted for the fast lane. Nevertheless, Melissa and I do hit upon several great teachers. And great showers.

One evening, while walking home from YogaWorks — skin lotioned up, hip flexors tweaked, ginger tea in hand — I pass a sight on Thompson Street that's so strange that I'm forced to stop. It's a shop called the Little Lebowski, exclusively dedicated to Jeffrey "the Dude" Lebowski, Jeff Bridges's character in the 1998 Coen Brothers film *The Big Lebowski*.

Stepping inside, I bump into a life-sized replica of Lebowski (yours for $400) — sunglasses on, hair over the shoulders. A sign behind him announces: *The Dude Abides*.

Browsing the Little Lebowski, I discover $27 T-shirts ("I'm the Dude, man"), alongside DVDs, posters, mugs, costumes, and action figures of the film's characters. Amid the aisles of merchandise is plenty of irony: a story about a guy who kicks back, smokes weed, and eschews capitalism has become a retail outlet.

At the front of the store, a middle-aged man sporting a Lebowski-reminiscent haircut speaks up as he sees me looking curiously in his direction. "I'm a Dudist priest," he tells me, "in the Church of the Latter-Day Dude."

"Excuse me?"

As if to explain, he passes me a copy of *The Dude Te Ching*. I listen for the sarcasm that never arrives. He's fun-loving but ultimately solemn about this. He abides, man.

It turns out he is one of 150,000 Dudist priests worldwide seeking to correct civilizational excess. "Lebowski is the most recent embodiment of Dudist mystics," he says, "going back to Lao Tzu and the Buddha, and continuing through Walt Whitman and Kurt Vonnegut." Then he turns his attention to a young woman who has just come through the door, and I return to the racks, weighing the $27 in my wallet against a rather cool "Abide" T-shirt. I'm tempted. I've watched *The Big Lebowski* three times over the years, long-intrigued by the character's rebel shrug, his annoyance with modernity, and his amusing approach to simple living. I hold the T-shirt up in front of a mirror, but then I remember Vicki Robin's "gazingus pins" — impulse buys that give a buzz of pleasure but little deep happiness. I put the shirt back.

As I'm leaving, the Dudist prophet is telling the new shopper: "Lao Tzu — you know, the founder of Taoism — did in fact say, 'Smoke 'em if you got 'em,' but he uttered it in ancient Chinese, so it was partially lost in interpretation."

Outside the Little Lebowski, I take out my Bolivian notebook and write: *The Dude abides.*

Walking home, I feel slightly outed. All our freebies feel too...Dudist. Those ripe mangoes Melissa and I wolf down — the rock-climbing gym and YogaWorks, the Guggenheim and Lincoln Center — are making my cheeks sticky. This doesn't feel like avoiding the rat race. It feels like mooching off it.

I'M AT THE UPRIGHT CITIZENS BRIGADE improv comedy show in Chelsea, sitting beside a longtime hero of mine, author and activist Vicki Robin. She's doubled-over in laughter and gripping my hand, thoroughly entertained by the team of twelve comedians creating a science fiction–themed skit.

Vicki is visiting New York from her home outside Seattle and suggested we meet here. In her sixties, she exudes freshness, humor, vitality — as her vise grip on my hand attests. I'm laughing, too, therapeutically so. Laughing the angst right out. I'm joyful, too, because my mom is here — stopping over for a night en route from Vermont to Chapel Hill — and so is Melissa. Plus, very Robin-esque, it cost just five dollars apiece for us to enjoy ninety minutes of some of the city's smartest comedy.

Vicki and I met a few years back, serendipitously, through the National Park Service. The agency invited us to give back-to-back talks at Yosemite's Tuolumne Meadows. She and I hiked the Yosemite high country together for two days before the program, and over the hours, I came to feel I was in the presence of a sagacious elder. She offered wisdom about resilience — to climate change, in our personal lives — and elucidated ideas that evolved from her million-copy bestselling 1992 book, with the late Joe Dominguez, *Your Money or Your Life*, which argues that too often we trade our precious hours of life for money, then use that money for things that bring little satisfaction. The book suggests reducing expenses to a level of "enough" — since both too little as well as too much are recipes for unhappiness. As personal expenses drop and savings grow, we have less need to work for money and more free time to focus on what we love.

Burdened with credit card debt after college, I followed Robin's practice of tracking every penny I spent in an account book each evening, and I was amazed to find that some 30 percent of my expenses were on "gazingus pins," or things that, in the end, I decided weren't worth the exchange of my life energy. I graphed it over the months, watching the line of expenses go down without a drop in the quality of my lifestyle. I paid off my debts and took a pair of scissors to my credit cards. I wasn't making a bundle after college as a junior high school teacher at a Native American school, nor later as an aid worker, but I always "paid myself first" before paying the other bills, depositing 10 percent of every paycheck into investments. Over time, I found myself living well below my means, a practice that eventually paved the way, financially, to our Slow Year in Manhattan.

At the comedy show intermission, Vicki exclaims: "Liberty? Is that really the name of Liberia's national currency?" I nod. "Trade some of your liberty for every purchase. Delightful!"

I put an arm around my mom's shoulder and another around Melissa's. Vicki is shining before us. She's always shining. She says: "A good question to always keep in mind: 'What's your joy-to-stuff ratio?' "

When my mom asks her to clarify, Vicki responds: "Each time I'm about to take out my wallet, I ask: How much joy will this purchase bring into my life relative to the 'life energy' I expend?"

This is the kind of pithy, useful insight that landed Vicki on my personal Wisdomkeeper Council of Elders. That's the little board of directors for my life. I began to form it a few years back, when it struck me how sad it is that we undervalue the acumen of our seniors. So now, a "council" of inspiring elders guides me philosophically — through how they live — and also through our conversations when I seek advice or a sounding board for decisions. Among them: my extraordinary parents, John de Graaf ("Take back your time, but not *all* of it"), David Abram ("We live in the E*air*th"), and Vicki.

SEVERAL DAYS AFTER VICKI RETURNS TO SEATTLE, I overhear something at Prodigy: "...and then yesterday we hit some forty galleries in Chelsea."

This tidbit snaps me out of my Dudist-priest-like gaze through the coffee shop's bay window. I'd been busy watching the leaves change color on the tree beside Unoppressive, Non-Imperialist Bargain Books; busy daydreaming over a dry-and-extra-hot cappuccino. But not too busy to eavesdrop. An art professor from Atlanta is describing some of the Chelsea galleries.

Forty galleries? Just a ten-minute stroll from our micro, under the High Line? Though I was aware of Chelsea as a contemporary art area, I didn't realize the bounty of art on tap for free viewing.

So, early one Thursday evening, Melissa and I play dress up and hit the Meatpacking District. Melissa dons a black dress and rainbow knit scarf, her hair in a retro bun. I've got on a beige jacket and ever-so-slightly ripped jeans. "I feel like we're acting," Melissa says, as we climb the stairs at Gansevoort Street up onto the High Line, a one-mile aerial greenway recycled out of the abandoned West Side Line spur of the former New York Central Railroad. We hold hands as we walk the pleasantly funky path of native plants through the linear park, taking in the railway track left exposed and the gleaming Hudson River below to the west, finally taking the stairs down into the Chelsea galleries.

At the Mitchell Algus Gallery on 25th Street, lyrical abstract artist Peter Young of Bisbee, Arizona, displays his mandala-inspired paintings. Melissa and I are sipping cups of free juice, which the gallery is handing out at the bar. I'm checking out a ten-by-ten-foot, intricate purple-and-yellow-themed mandala painting when something catches the edge of my gaze: a thin man in a panama hat, getting a beer at the bar.

Nothing too unusual about that. *Except* he'd been on line ahead of me at the bar five minutes ago, and didn't he already get a beer?

He strides my way, more swilling than sipping as he glances

at the paintings. Something's off about him. His aura doesn't scream Chelsea. The hat seems a bit over the top.

He stands next to me, also looking at the purple-and-yellow mandala. With two beers in five minutes, the Dude seems to be grazing a resource-rich environment. At Prodigy the other day, I watched a thirty-something woman order "one shot of espresso over ice in a big cup," then go to the self-service table and fill the cup with half-and-half. I later found out this is known in slacker circles as a "ghetto latte" — instead of six bucks for an ice latte, you pay two for the espresso and do-it-yourself from there.

"Nice painting," I say to the guy in the panama, whose second beer is now almost gone.

He studies me. "Outstanding," he says.

I don't know what else to say. He makes me uncomfortable. But I'm curious. Is he an alcoholic who, like Melissa and me, is playing dress up? Maybe he regularly does art openings for booze. As he's about to walk away, I say: "Cool about the free drinks, too."

He takes a slow swig of his beer, draining the bottle. "If you come to a fork in the road, brother, *take* it." He tips his hat, places his empty on a table, and exits the gallery door — perhaps off to another opening.

Time elongates. I'm frozen in front of the same mandala. The chatter filling the gallery sounds brasher, and my artista costume feels false. I spot Melissa across the crowd, taking in the beauty of a cluster of smaller mandala paintings. Taking in the beauty. *Taking it*. What are we contributing here? I'm feeling worse about my freeloading than I did after my visit to the Little Lebowski. As I find forks in the road — and take them

— somebody somewhere struggles to eat spaghetti with a spoon. It's not enough to abide. Slow is not about gaming the system. It's not about protecting one's mellow. It's not about me. There's something far deeper. It absolutely has to be about *us*.

THE NEXT DAY, I hit Bobst Library and delve more deeply into how our society dropped leisure from the national ethos. The freeloaders I've been meeting are rebelling against a society of Total Work, but the way they're doing it feels unfair and unproductive. I discover that, a century ago, American academics, journalists, and politicians were in a quandary about the imminent age of mechanization. As machines increasingly accomplished our tasks, the prevailing logic went, we would become unshackled from the eight-hour workday. This raised a big question about what the heck we would *do* with all of our free time. Some thought we might be able to create a new society based on something delicious: leisure. But how?

Of course, this future never materialized; the question was dropped. People simply used the time liberated through automation to do ever more. Never Stop Improving became the dominant ethos. So, for example, even as washing machines eliminated the toil of hand-washing clothes, hygiene standards stepped up, and we began to wash clothes, on average, twice as often. The overflowing laundry basket remains an enduring feature of contemporary life, to go along with the overflowing email inbox. Rather than giving us more free time to stroll the beach or play with our kids, our mechanical devices are themselves alluring time-drains, as we compulsively check them at all hours.

"I feel like I spend half my life breaking down cardboard

boxes for recycling," a harried lawyer friend tells me in his Brooklyn Heights apartment, while taking a utility knife to the Fresh Direct boxes that deliver all his family's groceries. Beside him is a mountain of other cardboard boxes — bearing gifts for relatives, diapers for baby, and a new food processor to cut chopping time.

"And the other half of your life?" I ask.

"Dealing with the crap that comes out of the boxes."

He's not unusual. Though he's a successful attorney pulling in a high salary, my friend still lives at the edge of his budget. The worry lines on his forehead reveal the beleaguering pace of his leisure-poor life, the same leisure-poor life that defines every economic strata of our modern world.

This is the precise conundrum I want to unravel in my Slow Year, and I am relying on some great minds for help. For instance, in her latest book, *True Wealth*, Boston College economist Juliet Schor presents case studies of twenty-first-century American households utilizing undervalued sources of wealth — like time, social relationships, and creativity — to escape from the work-and-spend cycle.

One chilly afternoon I'm on a bench in Washington Square Park, engrossed in *True Wealth*, which I have assigned to my students at NYU. In her section on creativity, Schor profiles people using "high-tech self-provisioning" to reduce market reliance by meeting core needs like income, food, housing, consumer goods, and energy through high-productivity technologies. These range from growing part of one's food (using permaculture); creating energy on a small scale (converting a Prius to a plug-in to double the gas mileage; putting up solar panels); and building homes with free labor (creating work

[margin, handwritten: True Wealth by Juliet Schor]

co-ops with neighbors). Then something grabs my eye: new "fab-lab" technologies — small, smart machines that make almost anything.

I look up from *True Wealth* at a few late-season Jammers making music, at William feeding Chico an almond. Are these machines the leisure-making, life-transforming technology experts anticipated a century ago? If we can program the 'bots to toil, could time wealth be more broadly extended across society?

I feel a tinge of hopefulness, despite the human track record, and hop the E train to a pop-up 3D-printing emporium in Midtown called 3DEA. I'm dumbstruck, watching a dozen turquoise-colored 3D printers in the store window as they diligently build items like high-heeled shoes and a model of the human brain. These clever prototyping machines are programmed to "print" things — in plastic, for example — layer by layer, until all the two-dimensional layers grow into a three-dimensional finished object.

True Wealth explains how the turquoise robots working in front of me were developed. They come out of MIT-pioneered "fab labs," short for "fabrication laboratories," which are "combinations of the essential machines needed to reproduce an entire lifestyle." Schor waxes about how the labs, designed for public use, are spreading across the globe and dropping in cost, empowering individuals "to produce almost anything." Using scrap materials and brainpower for the programming, she shows people deploying smart machines to make toasters, alarm clocks, furniture, computers, bicycles, clean energy, and even prefab, low-cost housing. In Afghanistan, they're making prosthetics. In India, they're working on solar devices.

But 3DEA is a different future. Scouring the emporium, I find little more than toy cars and "sexy objects" in the adults-only backroom. I head to the "3D Genius Bar" where customers can tell Dwayne their idea, and he'll program its creation. I tell Dwayne: "Please print something to save me time."

Dwayne inhales sharply, and his gaze floats to the ceiling. As he ponders, a bus races by outside on Sixth Avenue, the cloudless sky behind it 3D-printer blue. "Save you *time…*" he repeats.

I nod. Dwayne continues to ponder as customers buzz through the store, buying up what I'm realizing amounts to plastic kitsch. Finally, Dwayne smirks. "Thirty seconds to orgasm?" he suggests, nodding toward the 3D-printed toys in the adult room.

Maybe 3DEA is an anomaly. So, I hit MakerBot on Mulberry Street in the Village, another purveyor of 3D printers. Sadly, I find no Leisureologist's future here, either. The store is mostly geared to selling plastic-printed knickknacks and, of course, the company's own "next-gen" Replicator II 3D printer — for $2,199 — which certainly can't replicate itself.

MY STUDENTS ARE SKEPTICAL about 3D printing as a form of self-provisioning.

"Did you hear about the Wiki-Weapons Project?" Nicole says. "It raised $20,000 in an online campaign to promote *printable guns* to avoid firearms control."

I feel a chill in our classroom in the Woolworth Building today. "And though MakerBot deleted 3D-gun blueprints from its site," Nicole continues, "that did squat because a high-tech gunsmith firm has started open-sourcing its 3D-printed gun. You can print it overnight in 3D plastic!"

"That bites," JT says. "We just end up printing violence." Then he mumbles about how his parents, back in Iowa, bought a Roomba vacuum cleaner robot, but they still end up multitasking on work stuff while the thing vacuums. So it didn't, in the end, free up time.

Nobody else seems to want to talk. The energy in the room is low. Perfect. That provides a switch to flip.

I write on the whiteboard: *The significant problems we face cannot be solved at the same level of thinking we were at when we created them.*

"Einstein said that." I pause. "How does his thought relate to 3D printers and vacuum robots?"

Shifting in seats. A tentative hand inches up. "New technologies don't change things. They just let us do more of the same, and faster."

JT's hand goes up. I've noticed his analytical skills sharpening over the semester. "Einstein's saying we need to think at a different level," he says.

I write on the board: *paradigm shift*. Then I write a link to the 1997 essay "Places to Intervene in a System" by systems-thinking pioneer Donella Meadows, which Vicki Robin had recently sent me.

Together we tease out the hierarchy of nine places to intervene in the system with the goal of changing it — material stocks and flows, driving positive feedback loops, the rules of a system, the goals of a system — coming up with examples of each as a group. I feel the class energy rising. By the time we arrive at Meadows's final, ninth level, the one she says is the most effective level to operate on, but also the most difficult to achieve, the room feels like a symphony hall where the orchestra is reaching the end of the last movement. When I ask what that key final level is, one of the students has already zeroed in: "It must be paradigm shift. That's massive...but there's no higher level."

I break the class into pairs to discuss this one on one, and I circulate through their conversations. The way their neural pathways flip to solutions is a microcosm of the very paradigm shift we're talking about. Nicole enthuses to Vanessa about the Maker Faire convention she just attended. "There, you're not a brainless consumer of commercial rubbish. You're among thousands of self-provisioners creating in community." And JT, on the edge of his chair, says to Alvaro: "Have you heard what that fab lab in Iowa is doing? They're actually creating technologies — like lighter super-adobe and micro-hydroelectric wood-splitters — that are cheap to produce, and free us from wage slavery. It's a radical shift, but we need to find ways to think beyond this ecocidal paradigm that in the end is not really making us any happier."

"WHY DON'T YOU HIGH-FIVE THAT GUY?" I say.

"Who?" Melissa asks.

"The jogger in the green jacket, coming toward us."

It's a postpeak fall day, and we are walking the jogging path around the expanse of the Central Park Reservoir, which looks polished, a hand mirror turned skyward, reproducing the sky's colors and light. The browning leaves and grasses on the edge of the water are drained of vitality. Everything has already fruited and flowered.

Melissa laughs, shakes her head. "No way."

The jogger is still fifty feet away. I think to high-five him because it happened to me yesterday. While biking the Hudson River path through West Harlem in the late afternoon, I passed a group of four young African American women walking in the opposite direction. As I was about to coast by, the tallest stuck out her hand and yelled, "High-five!" Reflexively, my hand rose from the handlebar to meet hers. *Slap!* Our touch was the first human contact I'd experienced all day. I biked two more miles, then three, through Midtown and back into the Village, my palm still warm.

"Why not?"

Melissa flashes a skeptical look. On the glassy surface of the reservoir behind her, tiny black ducks bob alongside mallards and seagulls. The green-jacketed jogger approaches, and Melissa stops. She calls out, "Hello there...high-*five!*"

Seeing Melissa's extended palm, the man's face brightens. Stride unbroken, he raises a hand and meets hers with a solid clap.

Melissa lights up, too, effusing over how good she feels after doing it. "But he probably didn't get freaked out," she adds, "because I'm a woman."

"High-five!" I say to the next passing runner, a woman. Her perplexed look instantly softens, and her hand shoots up to meet mine. "Woo-hoo!" she calls out over her shoulder.

We deliver more high-five presents. There's not a grouch among the joggers. Everyone's hands and smiles meet ours.

We peel off the reservoir path, dropping into one of the forested sections to the west. There, thirty feet up in a tree, a barred owl sits. We locate him via the telescopic cameras and binoculars on the ground below. The birdwatchers inform us the large owl is resting from his southern migration.

"Where do they winter?" Melissa asks. The Caribbean? All the way to Bolivia? Nobody knows. The only thing certain is that, with the season changing, the owl won't be in New York for long. His mysterious, almost human eyes peer down at Melissa and me as we lean on either side of a pine tree, a calming practice David Abram suggests. Simply lean on any tree in the city, he says, and join the "more-than-human matrix."

I'm feeling relaxed. We continue to lean. A Latino family of six passes us, the boom box in Dad's hand sounding with a song I know. "Dos Gardenias," an old Cuban love song, popularized by the Wim Wenders film *Buena Vista Social Club*. I listen to the sweet melancholy of it fade as the family slips deeper into the park, and Melissa and I lean. My thoughts wander to the Wisdomkeepers who are guiding my Slow Year: to Abram, leaning right beside us; to de Graaf, who's started a new Seattle-Area Happiness Initiative (which he calls "SAY HI," for short); and to Vicki Robin.

Vicki told me after the comedy show that "her dwindling public" is "now in the tens of tens." Million-copy bestseller or not, she has yet to publish another book. When F. Scott Fitzgerald said that "American lives don't have second acts," perhaps he was talking in part about how our society only values the young and new, and people like Vicki tend to lapse into forgotten elder status.

As "Dos Gardenias" echoes through the trees, I feel something tingly and familiar happening. An idea in incubation. The story of *Buena Vista Social Club* is resurrection: Ry Cooder visits Cuba and plays with forgotten elder musicians. A new album dusts off the old *trova* music, becomes a hit, until, finally, the old-timers pack New York's Carnegie Hall. Could I, somehow, create a new hit record with de Graaf, Robin, and Abram? Put them in conversation with one another around some of the big questions of our day — as a way to bring *them* to a large audience in New York?

The idea Melissa and I spin out on the subway ride home is a little nuts. As a senior fellow in the World Policy Institute, a long-established think tank, I have a platform I can use, and I will in a quirky way: to host my Wisdomkeeper Council of Elders in a very big, very public powwow. Having come to a golden fork in the road, we'll use it to feed others.

10. THE SELF-PACED PLANET

NOW IT'S TIME TO WORK.

Ciao, Leisureology. I'm on a mission, a quixotic one: to spotlight these forgotten Wisdomkeepers through a high-profile New York City panel and in a VIP "Big Thinkers" workshop. I raise funds, pull together logistics, and lock in John de Graaf, Vicki Robin, and David Abram. *True Wealth* author Juliet Schor can't attend, so I organize a lecture for her on another date at the World Policy Institute. To replace Schor on the panel, my assistant and I rope in Colin Beavan — star of *No Impact Man*, a 2009 film about living carbon neutral in a New York City apartment. For the VIP workshop, we secure journalists from the *New York Times* and *Harpers*, academics from Columbia and NYU, and top investment bankers and foundation officials. It's thrilling. We'll get these big shots together with the Wisdomkeepers to reimagine the growth paradigm.

I work. On top of the NYU class, I have budgets to manage,

meetings to schedule, venues to reserve. One evening, I'm atop Tar Beach, bundled in a wool coat, pecking away at a laptop.

"Whoa!" Melissa says, when she comes up to the roof. "I've never seen you with one of those up here." She lifts an eyebrow. "What happened to *slow*?"

I snap the computer shut and rise to hug her. "I'm slow on the inside," I say.

The next morning, I eat an everything bagel on the Pier 45 lawn, watching the Hudson's effortless crusade to reach the Atlantic. That's how I feel. Effortless, even as my work expands. It's the flow state, where you are so engaged in the work that if someone were to interrupt you all of a sudden and ask what you're thinking about, the answer would be: nothing. Whether computer programming or landscaping, it's as if you're lost in an improv jazz riff. Neither thinking nor working, you flow.

Slow Work, it seems, is the opposite of my Queens-era workaholism. The stressed-and-addictive tug I felt in my "uni-moon" days has been transformed — even the phone calls and dreaded whiteboard planning feel playful. Still, to keep my old tendencies in check and stay accountable, I measure each min-ute of nonidling in my life in two neat columns at the back of my Bolivian notebook. I clock in at the start of each work activ-ity, however small, and clock out when it's complete or paused. After a few weeks I add things up. *Adieu*, seven-day weekends of summer. Farewell five-day weekends of spring. I'm back up to a thirty-two-hour workweek, or the equivalent of four eight-hour days.

That average soon includes an unanticipated workstream. Four New York artists, having read my book *Twelve by Twelve*, have designed an urban 12 x 12 interactive art piece, and together we secure foundation funding to build it. Then I'm asked to coordinate the project through the World Policy Institute: synchronize the creative team, build an interactive website, and line up eight artists to serve weeklong residencies in the 12 x 12.

Not wanting to disown the Leisure Ethic entirely, I maintain a hard limit of thirty-two hours of work per week, and I find myself using a pleasurable word a lot: *no*. No, I'm sorry, I can't do the press release. No, I'm unfortunately unable to meet on Sunday. No, I can't speak at that luncheon. Either others are found to do these things or, sometimes, they don't happen. This is experimental territory. I wonder: Will the practice of working "enough" — and then stopping to enjoy life — cut it in hypercompetitive New York?

Most of the time I forget about it and flow. I'm reminded of something our yoga teacher, the white-turbaned Amanbir, once said at Golden Bridge: "Do nothing and accomplish everything." I didn't get it at the time. But now, as I enjoy my bagel and watch nature effortlessly deliver a hundred million tons of water to the Atlantic, doing nothing, accomplishing everything, I'm beginning to understand. Indeed, the 12 x 12 is engineered, the artist residencies are filled, the website goes live — and while I help make it happen, I do so joyfully and without stress, all the while preserving abundant downtime. Like right now, on Pier 45's lawn, watching a beetle beside me imbibe a dew droplet from a blade of grass.

The thumb-sized insect inches forward in its shiny armor, antennae sweeping systematically, as if looking for hidden landmines. I place a scrap of everything in its path.

The bagel chunk sits centimeters from her antennae, but

Sister Beetle passes it by. As I continue to enjoy each bite of my breakfast and watch seagulls dive into the Hudson for theirs, I sink into a kind of *wu wei* ("alert inactivity") similar to the flow state I've been experiencing while working. Meanwhile, the beetle inches southward beside my torso. I pick up the Bolivian notebook and write: *Do nothing, accomplish everything.*

I place the bagel scrap in front of the beetle again. This time she stops. Her tiny antennae tap it once, then twice, then freeze.

I'm rapt. The beetle remains frozen. The Empire State Building, backlit by a rising sun, stiffly looks on. A hundred other skyscrapers attend to the beetle's next move. The seagulls abandon their fishing and now squawk overhead. A yellow-and-black New York Water Taxi sprints to the Pier 45 dock, horn proudly ablow, but the towers and the seagulls and I pay it no mind as we await Sister Beetle's next move.

Suddenly, unbridled debauchery. The beetle plunges her entire face — mouth, pincers, eerie insect eyes — into the soft dough. Then she bicycles herself yet deeper into the Answer she's found, into a heaven of boiled-before-baked

Jewish dough. I sink incisors into mine, appreciating the bagel's mouthfeel, then run a hand up my furred forearm, noticing our similarities. The beetle has limbs, too, though hers are closer shaved. We share eyes, a mouth, an abdomen, and a weakness for everything.

THE FOLLOWING MONDAY at 6 AM sharp, Melissa and I awake to her chirping phone alarm and find ourselves up-*up*town in the Natural City: a rustic camping lean-to in the fifty thousand mountainous acres of Harriman State Park. An hour Shortline bus ride north from Manhattan, it's even closer to us than some of the outlying subway stations.

Shedding my sleeping bag, I walk down the forest trail and fetch water from the creek. Then I rake down the coals from last night's bonfire, add firewood, blow the flames up, and boil water. "Morning," Melissa says, as I hand her a cup of coffee. The fire crackles before us in the quiet dawn as we munch muesli with almond milk. Then Melissa straps on her backpack, kisses me, and heads to work — via a mile by foot to the Tuxedo trailhead, the commuter bus to Grand Central, and a five-minute crosstown stroll to her building on 42nd Street.

Later in the day, as I'm romping in the woods alone, it strikes me for the first time that Melissa has commuted to her glass tower from a primitive lean-to. The fact that this didn't feel at all novel signals to me how seamlessly, over the past half year, we've intermingled nature with city. Our micro-apartment has a little public transit box holding more than just the Manhattan bus and subway maps; it also contains the LIRR, Shortline, and ferry schedules that cover the complete Natural City.

example for reading

That's what happened yesterday: we dipped into the box, found out the Shortline would get her to the UN on time, then packed quick bags and scooted out to sleep in the wilderness. As it turns out, it works. Melissa stealthily changes clothes in a restroom and arrives early for her first meeting. "The creek flowed through my day at the office," she tells me later, "and my whole day was infused with the smell of the forest."

The sun arches westward. Ten miles of hiking. Kundalini by a waterfall. Siesta on a soft bed of pine needles. Each pine cone and fallen antler, each ground squirrel and lily pond *belongs*. Nothing is extraneous in this wild organic mysterious forest, including me. After being in a civilization where I'm programmed to never be satisfied, how good it is to belong.

The sun is close to setting when I spy the day's first fellow tool-maker. Just a shape at first, hustling along far up the trail, in my direction. I'm feral after this mute day in the wilderness, joints oiled, muscles toned. The shape gets bigger, becomes female. Curly brown hair. A little while back I passed a sign indicating a scattering of cabins evidently grandfathered in to the state forest. This person — I see now she's middle-aged, in a gym suit — must be fast-walking to a cabin.

"Excuse me," she huffs, out of breath, when our paths cross, "but do you know what time it is?" Her face looks anxious.

I hold no timepiece, and I haven't spoken a peep since Melissa left at daybreak. "It's that time," I hear myself say, as I point to the orange blaze of sun melting into the ridgeline.

The anxiety on her face quadruples. She's not only late now. She's also alone, in the wild, with a lunatic. Backing away, she sputters, "It's just that...I hope I'm not...late for my ride. *Thanks!*" She pivots and fast-walks away.

Monday night in the lean-to. Off-season. Midweek. Alone. I listen to the few insects still chirping in advance of imminent winter, listen to the creek and the pop of a dying fire. The flames wink to black, and I slide into my sleeping bag in the lean-to, open my laptop, and start journaling about Manhattan. Bagels with a beetle on Pier 45. *I place a scrap of everything in her path.*

My fingers stop. The cursor blinks. I look up from the screen's glow into pitch-black woods. To a passing deer or bear, I'm huddled before a flame.

Fingers move again. *Her tiny antennae tap the bagel. There's a pause. I'm rapt.*

Though I'll log this toward my thirty-two-hour workweek — I'm on a laptop, after all — I'm not writing with a specific purpose in mind. This is a purple patch: a free-stream of prose that may later flow into a river that wants to make sense. But *this?* A hundred other things happened on Pier 45 last Wednesday. Hudson River droplets evaporating. Lovers quarrelling. A Rottweiler chasing down a cherry-red ball. Casting the loose fishnet of language into Manhattan, I haul in a bagel and a beetle. As a yellow moon cracks a Harriman ridge, I grasp something about writing. It's Slow. A writer's consciousness diffuses, through letters, across a film of thought, mingling with another's. Reading is Slow. The reader, deserting the work-a-day, somersaults into the slipstream of story.

"*SLOW* CITIES?" SAYS MY COLLEAGUE, Todd Jameson, a professor of advertising and marketing at NYU. He lays a skeptical look on me, across our open menus at an Irish pub near Wall Street. "Let's bracket that. Because first I'm going to tell you what I hate about flextime."

Todd is handsome, in his late fifties. He's lanky with curly chestnut hair. Like me he teaches just one class; he's also a full-time executive at a Madison Avenue advertising firm. Todd lives alone in a Midtown, Hudson-view penthouse. We met a few weeks back at a "new faculty" cocktail, and I decided to invite him to lunch in order to filter some new ideas — ones incubating in my class, my writing, and in the process of organizing the big Wisdomkeeper events, now just a week away. I'm upfront with Todd: we're from different worlds, and I'd like him to help me avert the insidious "confirmation bias" phenomenon, where we tend to filter into our lives only one type of information — the type that *confirms* our existing point of view.

"So I have this bitch of a colleague," Todd says, "who abuses our flextime policy — you know, where you can work whatever hours you want, as long as you get the work done. It's supposed to free you up, but it actually has the opposite effect."

"How so?" I gaze out over Todd's shoulder. The Irish Pub he chose for us is Slow. It's unfranchised, homey, flush with regulars. The owners' story is on the menu.

"So here's what Mrs. Machiavelli does: Goes to the *movies* at lunchtime and works *out*. But then, snake-like, she's on email late into the evening with the higher-ups and lower-downs when I'm unwinding. So when I jump on email in the morning, all these decisions already got made, rapid-fire, between like eight and midnight!"

"So working flextime really means... working all the time."

He nods. "If you're not on your iPhone until midnight, you're undercut." He shakes his head. "The upshot: I'm on the laptop till midnight every day, too."

A pleasant waitress takes our order. The bagpipe music

is low, the furniture agreeably unkempt. Men laugh over an afternoon Guinness at the bar beyond the unfashionable eighties glass partition. "Now. About this 'slow' thing," Todd says, passing his menu to the waitress. "Not feeling that. What positive words do you associate with 'fast'? We could come up with a hundred, right? Efficient, quick, enthralling, wild, fun. I could rattle off happy connotations straight through lunch." He cracks his knuckles. "But what are the positive associations for 'slow'?"

Todd forms his thumbs and pointer fingers into a rectangle and looks at me through it. "What you're really saying is 'self-paced,' right? Now *that* appeals. Twenty-first-century urbanites want more control over their time. Here you go: the Self-Paced City."

I'm liking Todd more and more. I imagine he's a well-loved professor, sparkling, as he does, with energy. "True," I say, "'self-paced' is part of it. But it's not just about autonomy."

Todd flips over his paper placemat, takes out a pen, and starts scribbling synonyms for *slow*, narrating his train of thought aloud. I join the brainstorm. He lists *relaxed* (too lethargic), *mindful* (too cliché), and *thought through* (not quite).

"How about *thorough*," Todd suggests. "No…wait a minute!"

On the placemat, he pens, in broad capital letters: MIND BODY BALANCE.

"Isn't that what we're really talking about? When I'm not stressed by work, I'm more efficient, and *happier*. MBB! That's it, Bill."

"But isn't there already Body Mind Spirit? BMS?"

Todd nods. "But maybe MBB's not copyrighted." He looks

at me, as if weighing what to say next. "Here's an open secret:
I'm going to give you the formula for how every single decision gets made in corporate America, i.e., America." Finding
his placemat filled, he grabs mine and flips it over. "This formula captures how the captains of industry think. The world's
Joe Schmos use it, too."

In huge letters, Todd writes: "I: H x S = $."

I stare, trying to decipher it. Todd sips his soft drink, then
explains: "I is the idea. Build a better mousetrap, send a letter
to Wichita, encourage people to work less and enjoy life more.
Whatever! H is how you do it, and S is the speed at which it gets
done. You with me?"

I nod. The food arrives — filet mignon for him; eggplant
parmesan for me — but Todd is so absorbed in his equation he
hardly notices. "We live in a universe of S. So, if you can show
that *reducing* S — the speed of doing something — benefits this
side of the equation" — he underlines the dollar sign five times
— "then people are still listening to you. But if it doesn't benefit
this" — now he circles the dollar sign over and over, so much
that his pen tears through the placemat — "then you're shit."

Theatrically, he drops the pen on the equation, pulls his
steak over, slices into it, and takes a bite.

His algebra may be wobbly, but Todd's point about the
almighty dollar is not. I'm increasingly apprehensive, thinking
about the pending de Graaf–Robin–Abram panel and the Big
Thinkers event. Will Wisdomkeeper ideas like gross national
happiness, "becoming animal," and the joy-to-stuff ratio be,
well...*shit* because they are not perceived to increase $?

Todd and I eat and continue to chat. I enjoy being with
him and admire the inventive mindset of his trade. But our

conversation also partly deflates my spirits. Dr. Meadows's ninth place to intervene in a system — the paradigm shift — seems even harder, and I'm craving a large slice of confirmation bias.

Outside the pub, before we part, Todd says: "Forget slow. You need to brand self-paced. You need to *own* self-paced."

"Own it?" I ask.

"Right. The Self-Paced Workday. Self-Paced *Diet*." Todd sticks out a hand, and a taxi pulls up. "Hell, the Self-Paced Planet."

FROM BEHIND A FLOOR-TO-CEILING WINDOW sixty stories up in a downtown penthouse, I look down into the lights of Manhattan.

"Hey," Melissa says, breaking my reverie. She's holding two crystal glasses of bubbly water. She hands me one, dipping a finger in hers and letting a drop fall to the hardwood floor. "*Pachamama*," she says, following the widespread custom in Bolivia, as we often do, of giving the first sip to Mother Earth. The practice feels strange this far from the ground.

We clink glasses. I'm still tingling with inspiration as my eyes jump around the hundred people mingling in the penthouse living room. We're here for a prelaunch fundraiser for one of the most ambitious legal actions in history. Some star trial attorneys just unveiled their plan: "We're going to sue the world's governments," one of them announced, "for damages to future generations by their inaction to stop climate change."

The rights of future generations. That's one of those illustrious paradigm shifts I keep bumping into. The idea is gaining legal ground, as these attorneys would have it, and they'll use it as a hammer to force governments to curtail their carbon emissions through carbon taxes, efficiency standards, and promoting green technologies. Generation Z is also in the house. By the baby grand, I see three teenagers from the iMatter campaign: youth claiming rights to a world without drowned coastlines and debilitating droughts. One of the teens just announced a Million Kids March to occur in DC in the spring. "We'll *demand* intergenerational rights to a healthy planet," he said.

Melissa and I snatch appetizers from one of the trays spinning through the room and sidle over to James Hansen, NASA's chief climate scientist. He's a renegade in the US government for his public calls for a drastic reduction in our carbon use, and I'm delighted to meet him. I lap up what he tells Melissa and me about the latest research from Greenland on glacial melt and about the urgency of this lawsuit against the world's governments.

Hansen eventually peels away to meet-and-greet others, and it occurs to me that he, the iMatter teens, and these visionary lawyers are sending out what Annie O'Shaughnessy calls "soul flares."

A soul flare is what happens when someone shines
    his or her light, no matter
what it is. In a song, a smile, a well-made soup;
    they send out a flare of light
that inspires others to shine their own.

I think of the flares that Robin, de Graaf, and Abram might send out in the big event tomorrow.

Tomorrow. I'm nervous. This is untried terrain, in two

ways. First, there's the imaginative ideas and policies, some of which heretically fail to raise $. And second, there's the hands-off manner in which I've been organizing the events.

Four-day workweeks. That's a lot for a Slow Year, but little for the American ethic. Sure, I've *felt* in the flow — doing enough and accomplishing plenty — but what if the Wisdom-keepers events flop? Modern life's eat-or-be-eaten ethos keeps most New Yorkers working like crazy to deliver a bigger crowd and hypermaximize impact. I think of the Todd Jamesons of the city, working until midnight to keep up, and also of the organizers of this killer legal effort, one of whom told me earlier: "We've not slept for three weeks to kick this baby off."

When I mentioned I had a big event tomorrow, she exclaimed: "And you're *here?*"

I told her a bit about the Leisure Ethic — finding balance between *otium* and *negotium* — and noticed her becoming uncomfortable. "So your work ethic is, what…minimum input, maximum output?"

I shifted feet. "That's the theory."

THE BIG NIGHT ARRIVES.

In six minutes I'm supposed to moderate a panel, here at the celebrated Demos think tank in Midtown, in joint sponsorship with the World Policy Institute. But I'm secreted away in a dim backroom.

"Showtime!" Melissa says, finding me. She studies my face. "What's wrong?"

I look away from her and out the window into a mile of red taillights. Four lanes of cars grind down Fifth Avenue below. Burning fossil fuels. Leaning on horns. Impatient.

I feel a soft hand on my shoulder. "It's packed in there," Melissa says.

I nod. *Four minutes to curtain.* Through the cracked door I hear the din of conversation and motion. The turnout is far better than we imagined. People will have to stand in the back.

"But what if they laugh the Wisdomkeepers out of the room?"

"They've come because they're *hungry*. For new ideas. And practices."

Ten thousand cars in traffic. The congestion and stress below resonates with my nerves and self-doubt. "How in the world are we ever going to change *that*?" I point out into Fifth Avenue. "Maybe Todd's right. We should brand Self-Paced. Own Self-Paced. Meet people where they're at."

Melissa straightens my collar. "Remember what George Bernard Shaw said? 'The reasonable man adapts himself to the world; the unreasonable one persists in trying to adapt the world to himself. Therefore, all progress depends on the unreasonable man.' This event is unreasonable. It's progress."

One minute. "You'll be great," she says, squeezing my hand and disappearing through the door.

Employing a Broadway performer's trick, I shake my hands vigorously overhead for thirty seconds. This gets the nerves out. My arms flop down, and I squint out into the traffic, blurring the taillights into an elegant red lava flowing as effortlessly as the Hudson. Everything out there on Fifth Avenue was dreamed up by somebody.

None of it has to be, I tell myself. We can create something else.

11. FLAMES ON THE HUDSON

A FAMILIAR FACE POPS OUT of the Fifth Avenue crowd of strangers waiting to cross 79th Street. The Met's façade looms, Melissa's hand in mine. "Bill!" calls the tall, chestnut-curled man as he draws near. "Amazing event last week."

We shake hands. At the VIP roundtable, Jerry was a private sector representative — one of the business insiders off of whom to bounce some less-than-mainstream ideas. "There are so few spaces where the likes of us finance types get to actually think beyond the box," he says to Melissa and me, "and actually brainstorm with others who are way *beyond* our own box. We should keep that conversation going."

Melissa and I climb the stairs to the Met, my spirits boosted by Jerry's firm handshake and honest smile. The energy of the Wisdomkeepers event felt good, but I wasn't quite sure what impression everyone walked away with. This spontaneous interaction makes me hopeful that all that *talking* about new ideas might actually catalyze something more profound.

Once inside the museum, Melissa and I find a secluded corner in the third-floor niche housing Chinese Decorative Arts. My head rests in her lap.

I chuckle. "There were some good moments. De Graaf declaring Thomas Jefferson's birthday as national 'Pursuit-of-Happiness Day.' "

"And David Abram," Melissa says, "pushing us to reconsider the wisdom of moving from ownership to 'usership,' like car- and appliance-sharing. When he said we're not materialistic *enough*, I think he was saying that we should appreciate the things in our life more. That shook things up."

Suddenly, I feel something. Expectantly, I touch the place where my cheek meets Melissa's belly. "Was that...?"

She laughs. "Just my stomach growling." We're alert for Squeaker's first kick.

We continue to idle in the noiseless Chinese Decorative Arts, talking a bit then falling quiet, allowing rare silence to penetrate this hallowed space. The burgundy cherrywood of the walls and ceiling glow in the soft light and remind me that it too was once alive. The Met is not just any museum. It's a place that brings the nexus of religion, history, spirituality, tradition, and creation into a space to simply be. Instead of reading all the little tags and memorizing dates and names, we've come to just *be* here and feel its sacredness echo around us.

I doze as Melissa runs her slender fingers through my hair, gently massaging my scalp. It's a big change to have her with me on a Slow Thursday afternoon. It's part of a shift she's been making with work. She convinced her boss to give her more work-at-home time when she has specific writing projects. It turns out Melissa is more productive in four or five hours of distraction-free time at home than she is in nine hours in the office — when chitchat, protracted meetings, and the commute are factored in. Plus, her efficiently finishing up work responsibilities allows us to countercyclically idle away some afternoons together.

Leaving Decorative Arts, we roam the Met without any particular plan, passing through some of our favorite spots — the Astor Court Chinese scholars' garden, Frank Lloyd Wright's linear living room, the back of the museum that parallels Central Park, the sun-drenched Modern Art wing. Eventually, we stop in front of an enormous Jackson Pollock painting. The work has no central focus, no foreground, no background. Pollack splashed and drizzled a range of color over the vast canvas.

Unrushed, we pass a quarter hour with Pollock. A tour group dips in, and I listen to the guide explain that Pollock's message is that our postmodern world is chaotic. "There is no center," she says.

As my eyes survey the splashed paint, I watch my mind: it wants a center, but finds none in the painting. I think of the new study in which a team of Stanford scientists calculated that we're changing the climate at a rate ten times faster than any point in the last 65 million years. Yes, we may be in a naturally occurring warming period, but our carbon-based industry is accelerating the shift by an astounding factor of ten. My eyes stray through the centerless colors. I think of James Hansen's book on climate change, *Storms of My Grandchildren*, and that unsettling title makes me worry about what this boiling world will be like, fifty years from now, for Amaya's and Squeaker's children.

A familiar powerlessness nudges in, the hair-thin roots of negativity. To starve the roots, I choose a *drisde*, or meditational focus point, a red dot at the top of Pollock's canvas. That dot is Melissa and me.

When my calmed eyes at last depart the *drisde*, they're no longer astray. The blue flecks beside us are Vicki Robin, Abram, and de Graaf, and the emerald splatters Hansen and Juliet Schor. The iMatter teens — a hundred milky splatters to our left — march on Washington as the purple pro bono trial attorneys sue for intergenerational rights. The fuchsia and pink swirls are Monica and Bruce and the Jammers, and the leaping blues are the high-five girls on the Hudson bike path. Our urban sanctuaries — the Rambles, Brooklyn Grange, Pier 45, Harriman — burst in emerald green. *Create the center.*

Suddenly, Melissa grabs my hand and pulls it to her belly. My eyes, wrested from our colorful community, meet hers. For a minute we're just looking at each other, and then I feel an unmistakable jabbing: Squeaker's first kicks.

MELISSA AND I AND OUR NEWEST VISITOR — forty-year-old Londoner Nick Buxton, a good friend from our Bolivia days — hit a candlelit Jones Street jazz bar called Café Vivaldi and excitedly catch up over hot wine. We haven't seen Nick since our small wedding in Melissa's hometown, Santa Fe, a year back, and we are thrilled to host him in the micro en route to a conference he'll attend upstate. An unbelievable jazz ensemble soon seduces us out of our conversation. Before long nobody in the packed joint even whispers. Piano, sax, trumpet, genius.

"Bloody brilliant," Nick says, when the musicians finish their set and coolly mingle into the crowd.

On our circuitous stroll over, we passed a half dozen other jazz clubs in the several square blocks around our apartment: Blue Note and the Village Vanguard, Fat Cat and One Step Down. Live music spilled out of them into the chill October evening. "Your neighborhood is a musical place," Nick says, as we toast in front of Café Vivaldi's fireplace. "I'll bet Greenwich Village, a century ago, also resounded with music — but maybe it was lutes and fiddles instead of saxophones. The soul of a particular city neighborhood gets passed down. Like urban genes."

Nick talks about a neighborhood on the bank of the Thames in South London. Over a century ago it was the seedy, working-class, politically radical ferry launch into greater London. "But, do you know, when I went back there recently, I noticed it still maintains that radical spirit...even though it's now very much on the Tube and part of greater London. City neighborhoods have their DNA."

The following morning, Nick and I stroll through Washington Square Park. The park has her makeup on, her maples and oaks daubed with auburn and peach. My NYU class starts in an hour, and I've invited Nick as a guest speaker. He's an analyst at the Transnational Institute, a Brussels-based NGO-network focused on the Global South — the "developing" nations of the southern hemisphere — and I know the students will enjoy him. We stop just east of the chess players to watch a park fixture: the dual-trumpet player, howling through his pair of horns like an assertive alpha elephant. Amazed, Nick starts to film the spectacle with his phone, but the musician immediately drops tusks and bellows, "Noooo videotaping!" The audience chuckles. Nick bows deep and pockets his phone.

Ten minutes later, by the fountain, a singing choir ambles our way. Two dozen white robes ripple in the wind, and they're conducted by a priest who walks backward in front of them. He wears a traditional black suit and white Roman Catholic collar and has poofed hair and blue-blazing eyes. It's Reverend Billy and the Church of Stop Shopping.

The best guerrilla theater movement to hit New York in years, Reverend Billy and his flock of talented singers compose and sing songs that question materialism and propose alternate values. *Grow food in organic city gardens!* the choir declares as it claps, sings, and strolls our way. *Delight in belonging, not belongings!*

They halt at the fountain. Nick and I join the huge crowd that immediately encircles them. A couple hundred of us clap along as the chorus completes a gospel tune. Then Reverend Billy delivers a sermon, beseeching and gesticulating like an old-time preacher. *Mayor Bloomberg is handing over parks like Washington Square to multinational sponsorship!* (Groans from the crowd.) *He's turning our pleasantly funky city parks into domesticated corporate spaces...with their advertising!* (Hisses, boos.)

Billy lets silence build as he dramatically runs his fingers through his outrageous hair and shakes his head in faux disbelief. "What's the name of the chain shuttering our local coffee shops?" he asks.

"Starbucks!" someone calls out.

"Amen, sister," Reverend Billy says softly, as the choir begins a slow build. They're humming softly now, and swaying, and snapping their fingers. The reverend sways with them, nodding as he exclaims, "The devil plans to franchise his evil brew a few blocks from here, pushing out more of our holy homegrown."

More boos and hisses.

The choir's snapping turns to clapping, and humming grows louder. "But does the devil know..." the preacher says, his voice quaking as it crescendos, "that he is *un*wanted...in... *Greenwich VILLAGE*?"

The crowd goes totally berserk. The choir now rips out in open-throated passion, decrying the coffee chain. Reverend Billy, now inflamed, gropes his way through the crowd, brushing past Nick and me. He grabs the wrist of an unlucky onlooker at the back. Quite unlucky, in fact, because he holds in his hand a Starbucks coffee cup.

Reverend Billy pulls the horrified guy back through the crowd and deposits him center stage, in front of the choir — then yells out that the exorcism begins!

Billy gesticulates over the cup, attempting to coax the devil out. The choir sings and the audience cheers on the exorcism in the kind of fun, countercultural energy I've come to love about our neighborhood. The guy with the coffee finally smiles and shrugs. Evidently deciding to join the winning team, he pours the beverage onto the pavement.

Crowd, chorus, and priest cheering him on, the man then puts the Starbucks cup on the pavement, lifts a heel, and crushes it.

"HEARD OF REVEREND BILLY?" I ask in my NYU class a half hour later. We've circled up desks; Nick sits to my right. About half the class raises hands, a few grins. "Why do you think he's exorcising Starbucks cups?"

JT, who has come to make a kind of religion out of anthropologist Arturo Escobar and relates almost everything to his innovative ideas, says: "The Church of Stop Shopping reminds me of Escobar. It's ordinary people challenging a corporate discourse of 'progress' and 'modernity' embodied by Starbucks."

"But they make good lattes," says Carlos, our Argentinian provocateur.

"Get real!" Nicole practically chokes out. "As if local places like Prodigy and Ninth Street Espresso don't make *better* coffee!"

Carlos puts hands in front of his face and feigns injury.

"And anyway," Nicole continues, "the local joints' profits stay in our neighborhoods instead of being drained out for advertising and executive salaries."

Nick then bridges the discussion to our topic for the day: climate change. It's his current research focus at the Transnational Institute. "Rounded local cultures are not the only things flattened by a dangerous 'progress' discourse," he says, in his soft London accent. "So's the biosphere."

For a half hour Nick lays out the latest science and global politics of climate change. His deadpan manner captivates the class, particularly when he lays out the "new math" of climate change based on research by European climatologists, recently popularized by activist Bill McKibben. "It's all about three numbers," Nick says. "First: 2-degrees Celsius. That's the limit all of the world's governments, in Durban, agreed is the maximum increase in average temperature the planet can absorb while still being comfortable for humans." The second, he says, is 514 gigatons. That's how much carbon we can burn and remain in the 2-degree limit. And third, 2,467 gigatons:

that's the amount of fossil fuels already discovered, not yet out of the ground, but already on the balance sheets of the world's oil companies.

Nicole's expression is appalled. She says: "The petroleum firms aren't going to leave 80 percent of their assets in the ground!"

Nick puts his whiteboard marker down and sits. He looks out into a silent circle of students. "That's the dilemma," he says. "They won't. Not without one of the biggest fights in history."

"But you don't *feel* global warming," JT finally says. "It's a slow-motion catastrophe. Humans will only change if it gets excruciating."

"We're starting to feel it," Nick says. "Droughts and forest fires in the American West; Katrina in New Orleans. And think of Manhattan, a low-lying island facing an ocean. Amsterdam has invested billions of Euros in dikes to protect it from storm surges. How much has New York invested?"

Zero.

A STORM IS COMING.

Weather reports are predicting a big one for the weekend. But I don't *feel* it.

In fact, we heard similar warnings last year, when Melissa and I were in Queens. Everyone dutifully stocked their houses with food and candles, even sandbagged their basement doors, but Irene didn't do much. Power outages. Some homes and vehicles crushed by falling trees. That's about it. Plus, New York is not New Orleans. None of it is *below* sea level, so a Katrina wouldn't be a Katrina here.

A storm is coming, but the day glistens as my wife and I look out from Pier 45 over the smooth Hudson. The Lackawanna clock tower in Hoboken is as crisply detailed on the water as above it. The only thing dimpling the surface calm are the casts of an older Chinese couple, whom I often see here, fishing for blue crabs. "They know how to live," Melissa says. "Outside, doing something meditative and practical."

I hug into Melissa's warmth, feeling one of Squeaker's now-frequent pokes, watching the couple. Their pants pockets are filled with little bells that chime when they move between their half-dozen freestanding fishing poles. They've clipped bells onto each of the pole tips, and they ding when a crab tugs below. The old woman pulls up a small crab. Her husband draws another one, equally small, through the calm, lake-like surface. I walk over and peer into their bucket. "You eat those?" I ask the man. "Yeah, yeah," he answers in passing, his pocket of bells jingling.

Melissa and I leave the Chinese couple to their crabbing and walk toward the vaulting white Bedouin tent at the tip of Pier 45. We lean, Abramesque, against two of the dozen trees planted at pier's end, watching a water taxi grinding by, the ever-more-tightly southern-arching sun diving headlong into Jersey City, as if hastening winter along. To get the energy out, I swing from a tree branch. Melissa joins me. We laugh, swing, and struggle with pull-ups as the sun dissolves.

THE NEXT DAY, I walk to the Washington Square Arch for an impromptu get-together with Brock and Fliss. I haven't seen them since I bailed on the Central Park wild food harvest. Though I'm late, there's no sign of them. I look up at the arch. The hawk, Bobby, is no longer around. Gossip has it he's migrated. Flown south, along with the monarch butterflies, the Vs of Canada geese crossing the harbor, and the four distinct warbler species temporarily alighting in the Tar Beach tree canopy. Eventually, I see Brock and Fliss walking toward me, holding hands. Fliss waves as they pass a guy making a mandala with fistfuls of colored sands.

We hug and sit on the lawn. It's wonderful to catch up. They're obviously an item, and Brock seems a little different, Fliss-contagion chipping into his workaday armor. His posture seems softer, and he speaks a little more from the heart and less from irony. And Fliss? It's not that she's less...feral. But she chooses her words a bit more carefully and hangs on Brock's often cerebral observations.

The wind picks up, sending leaves down on us. We acknowledge the topic *du jour*: the predicted hurricane. "We're going to get slammed," Brock says. "If not by this one, then the next."

Fliss snatches a falling leaf out of the air. "I am *glad* a big one is coming!" she says, crumpling the leaf up. "This city needs more...*weather*."

Brock starts talking about what Manhattan was like one million years ago, during a previous ice age. He points past the arch to the Empire State Building, saying, "The goddamn glaciers were *four times* higher than the Empire."

Before we part, I ask Fliss what she'll do now that moonlight bodysurfing season is over.

"Trim pot for Colorado again," she says, then punches Brock's shoulder. "Maybe I can convince *this* guy to join me." Brock smiles.

"Or maybe," Fliss adds, "I'll migrate further south, outrun the cold."

That evening, wind gusts in the trees over Bleecker Street as Melissa and I stroll to a much-anticipated splurge at Smörgås Chef, a Scandinavian gourmet place. We arrive to find the restaurant is nearly empty. The city is in hunker-down mode. The storm is still over the Caribbean someplace, but now it has a name: Hurricane Sandy.

A predicted storm, however, is not something you taste. Fennel soup, Swedish meatballs, and cured salmon on potato croquettes — *is*. For the dozenth time in Manhattan, Melissa and I are slow-chewing one of the best meals of our lives. I have one of those feelings, more frequent each week, that we're destined to grow old in the West Village. Like the beetle that sank itself into that soft bagel, we're burrowing into Manhattan. It's a dilemma that other urban friends have expressed, from San Francisco to Singapore, Portland to Paris. Habituate to urban sensorial variety, and anywhere lower-key can feel anticlimactic.

Flush with Scandinavia, we walk home via Pier 45. West 10th, Christopher, Bleecker, Morton. These are our streets, the ones we walk and bike every day. The subway in its tunnel is our car in the garage. Rockaway is our oceanfront. The Metropolitan Museum of Art is our living room. *New York* is our living room. Our micro-apartment doesn't feel minor anymore. It's our nest-perch in a city where we've made it, in part because it's a place we are, in tiny ways, helping to make.

There's wind on Pier 46. We stop here, something I haven't ever done. This is the truncated, Astroturfed younger cousin of our beloved Pier 45 next door, which juts much farther out into the Hudson.

We only stop here because of the bagpipe player.

She is red-haired, in her early twenties, and dressed in full Celtic duds. The fish-fin of her bagpipe swells and falls with forlorn music, the instrument's bladder inflating blowfish-like against a dark gleaming Hudson. A storm is coming.

The West Side Highway exhales beside us, its lights winking to red, traffic halting. I pull my wool coat close as the evening chill deepens. The bagpipe's mournful half notes blend with the rippling water illuminated by waterside buildings. The lit-up ripples look like candles bobbing, aflame, on the Hudson, reminding me of last year on 9/11.

I was walking the Hudson, farther south, near the Ground Zero site, when I happened upon a group of shaved-headed Buddhist monks in orange robes. In silence, just after sunset, they lit candles, placed them on minirafts, and launched them into the river. The candles' light dimmed as they bobbed slowly south, just as anger and fear recede into time's flow. The monks didn't explain their gesture; they didn't have to. The feeling was as wide and deep as the sound of this woman's bagpipe. The tempo picks up, merging with the growing sea winds.

The music stops.

Midtune. It's abrupt. The Empire State Building rises behind the musician like a long pipe from her instrument. The Hudson splashes on the pylons beneath us, and the highway roars again. She adjusts her kilt and looks to the sky.

FRANKENSTORM (N): twenty-first-century hyperstorm exaggerated by the heat-trapping gasses released into the atmosphere by human industry.

When Melissa and I depart early the next morning — on

the cheap-o Bolt Bus to Cape Cod, via Boston — we've yet to hear this new coinage. *Frankenstorm.* We're not leaving the city to flee Sandy. We'd planned the trip well before we heard about the storm. Just a long-weekend escape to Melissa's family's old summer place in the bayside village of Barnstable, to return Monday night.

At Boston's South Station, we switch to a local bus to Barnstable and walk the final mile to the clapboard house. I drop my pack and bike down Scudders Lane to Barnstable Harbor. The wind is blowing at twenty-five knots, and to beat the hurricane, I quickly dig oysters to shuck for dinner and receive a surprise bluefish. A fisherman, getting in his last surf casts before the rain, offers it to me. "Blues are too oily," he says, complaining about the absence of striped bass this year. I grill up the thirty-two-inch blue with butter and lemon. As Melissa and I dine, the wind screams in pulses through the shutters, a hyperventilating sky.

Then, *ʒap!* The electricity dies.

By candlelight, we listen to the storm shake the old house, and at night, the sound constantly awakens me. At 3 AM I descend the creaky stairs and step out onto the back porch, sticking a hand beyond the eave, letting the rain pelt it. I examine a single raindrop on my fingertip. Climatologists note that it might not come back as a raindrop again for another thirty thousand years. That's how long it could take for these particular molecules to circulate through the water cycle. Thirty thousand years on my pointer finger. It makes me appreciate the companionship of water this year, from Hudson kayaking and Rockaway surfing to the Harriman streams and cooling Tar Beach drizzles. But now, with the power out and a wind

gust sending a sheet of rain onto the porch, drenching my paja-
mas, water seems a little sinister, somehow. "The climate system is an angry beast," climatologist Walter Broecker once put
it, "and we're poking it with sticks." I strip off my cold, wet
clothes, wondering what's happening back in New York.

In the morning, the awful news begins to filter in. We are
without television, so it arrives piecemeal through phone calls.

The subways are flooded and inoperative.

Millions of New Yorkers are without electricity.

The UN is shut. NYU is shut, some of its buildings
swamped out.

Death toll is at a hundred and climbing.

"Oh my fucking God," Brock says to me over a staticky
phone line. "It's as surreal as when the planes hit the towers.
I'm a refugee from my own apartment. The thing is flooded
out, the elevators don't work, there's no power." His voice goes
fuzzy for a minute, and then I hear him saying, "...everybody's
walking around like zombies on Sixth Avenue, and there's no
public transportation —" Before I can ask him about Fliss, the
call drops.

Fliss. She's still living out in Rockaway. I can't get through
to her on the phone. I call Peter at the D. Piper Inn, where
Melissa and I stayed, and he tells me the Rockaways have
"taken it up the rear" with a half million dollars in damage to
his inn. Thousands of cars have been lifted by the waves into
heaps, along with chunks of the famous Rockaway Boardwalk.

The boardwalk. That miles-long stretch where we'd
watched for dolphins and biked — it's more than simply damaged by Sandy. It's *gone*. Swallowed by the Atlantic. Farther
up the Rockaway Peninsula, the lovely Kennedy's Restaurant,

where we recently ate, is *gone*. Swallowed by the rising Atlantic. And a hundred homes around Kennedy's have burned to the ground because firefighters couldn't reach them over the storm-trashed roads. Eleven people in the Rockaways are confirmed dead. I call Fliss again, but still nothing.

Melissa and I can't return to New York. Buses aren't running. Amtrak isn't either. NYU, and her office at the UN, remain shuttered. Our three-day weekend turns into eight, then nine. Unable to go home, I remember a woman from the Maldives, Ursula Rakova, one of the world's first climate-change refugees. I met her at the UN two years back. She'd traveled to New York to tell the world that the two thousand people in her village had to be evacuated to higher ground, their village drowned. I never thought, when I met Ursula, that I'd ever share her predicament, even temporarily. When email comes back up, I contact my students. "We're like refugees up in the Bronx," JT writes back. "Seven of us squatting in a one-bedroom apartment, sharing one shower."

BACK AT OUR COLD CORNELIA APARTMENT, I open the refrigerator and am slammed with a stench like road kill. Our building went nine days without electricity — it came back on just a few hours before our return — and everything inside the fridge is rotten. While Melissa tries to find the superintendent about restoring heat, I cover my nose and empty the refrigerator into the trash.

Up on Tar Beach, I break down the branches Sandy knocked from the tree onto the roof. I carry them down into the apartment to light a fire in our small fireplace. Melissa and I huddle silently in front of it, and I'm thinking about the shock of returning to Manhattan on the bus this afternoon. Trucks distributing free food, the malaise hanging over a tired city whose power is still out in many neighborhoods. Our apartment neighbors, looking harried, as if they'd aged a year, talking about the awfulness of the past nine days, living in a metropolis increasingly stinking of accumulating trash, without electricity, without public transport. Now, by the warm fire, it makes me feel a little guilty that Melissa and I were able to sit it out on the Cape while they huddled in dark micros.

Melissa buses to work the next morning because the downtown subways remain closed, and I wander down through an altered Washington Square Park. Barricades cordon off the tree limbs ripped down by Sandy. I see neither pigeons nor squirrels; hear no music. The park has never felt this silent. Doodletown silent.

Pier 46 on the Hudson, where the bagpiper played, is wrecked and fenced off. Pier 45 was also trounced by the surging waters, its wooden benches torn out, the Bedouin tent heavily sagging, parts of its railings carried away. This damage is but a sliver of the estimated $30 billion Sandy will cost the city. The Frankenstorm shakes up Mayor Bloomberg so badly that he appears on TV and announces he's switching his presidential endorsement from Romney to Obama because "at least President Obama acknowledges the problem of climate change." Bloomberg's switch seems to prove something one of my students said in class: people must feel disaster in order to change. However, standing alone on the broken tip of a Greenwich Village pier, all I feel is numb.

12. BRONX RIVER BOTTOM

"I QUIT MY JOB," Brock tells me. We're standing amid the rubble out at Rockaway. I've come to witness the damage to my favorite beach neighborhood in person.

My eyes widen. "Really?"

"I've had it. First came the financial meltdown. We *know* who caused it — thousands of greedy bastards in the banks and insurance firms and ratings agencies — but did they go to jail? No! I share offices with the same people, and they're richer than ever. It stunned me that Americans didn't go ape shit about it. We all just shrugged."

He looks out into the street, where a tangle of boardwalk planks entomb an overturned SUV. "And now *this*. Ultimately, our oil addiction caused Sandy, but people shrug and go back to work. They're scared, I know. I was scared to quit, too. But fuck it."

I ask him what he'll do.

"Head as far south as I can get. With Fliss. I've got savings."

South. I picture them in Bolivia. I picture Amaya. When I called her from the Cape, she sounded worried. "Are you okay, Daddy?" she asked, having seen the images from New York on television. I'm hit with a strong urge right now to hug her, to tell her I'm okay in person.

"Gotta split," Brock says, interrupting my thoughts. "Fliss awaits."

She's volunteering up in Breezy Point through the relief movement Occupy Sandy. She's helping people get back in their homes, and Brock is going to join her. I should join them, too, but I still feel too numb. I need to just walk Rockaway's ruins today. Take in this new world.

"Are you guys in love?" I ask, before Brock goes. "I mean, do I get matchmaking credit here?"

He pauses. "Fliss has this story. I think it's Buddhist. And it captures the honesty I love about her, and something about the way I'm going to start living."

"What's the story?"

He looks out to the ocean and says, "The journey of life is like rowing a boat to the middle of a large lake. Then the boat sinks."

I wait for him to continue. He doesn't. "That's the story?"

Brock nods. "That's it."

I'D HOPED TO FEEL INSPIRED atop the Brooklyn Grange rooftop organic farm with my Sustainable Development students. But I don't.

"Our beehives didn't make it through Sandy," Robert, the farm manager, tells us, his voice dejected. "They got ripped off the roof."

The chickens had to be relocated, too. Gone is the lively clucking and buzzing. And with the growing season over, the landscape is now one of dry brown vines and windswept husks. "It seems a little...dead up here," Nicole tells me, sounding disappointed.

I try to bolster her spirits, describing the lush eden of my summertime visits. In response, Nicole coughs. So does JT. Several of the students caught colds during their evacuation from downtown dorms and apartments. They lived in squatter's conditions in the Bronx and elsewhere Uptown, areas farther from the more damaged, ocean-facing downtown.

Beyond New York, even my Wisdomkeepers are uncharacteristically in the dumps for other reasons. "Lyme disease," David Abram tells me. He's got it, and bad. He's been trying various treatments but now aches a lot of the time. Picturing the author of *Becoming Animal* with Lyme disease strikes me as ironic and tragic. Equally as tragic is that Lyme disease — with more recorded cases every year — is making people all along the Eastern Seaboard scared of being outdoors at all, yet another distancing between people and nature. Fear of a debilitating disease can push you to extremes.

De Graaf, too, is down. "Take Back Your Time has little money left," he tells me on the phone. He describes how the right-wing Heritage Foundation and Ayn Rand Foundation are doing big things like "distributing thousands of copies of *Atlas Shrugged* for free on college campuses. They're trying to change the paradigm, but toward *more* hyperindividualism instead of more community." He further laments, "And the progressive foundations only fund little projects, those with 'measurable results.' But those interventions are too small to change the culture a decade or two down the line."

Meanwhile, Melissa and I have become frustrated with her prenatal care. Because Melissa has good insurance through her job, we're lucky to be at an Uptown New York hospital. But like most hospitals, they view pregnancy as a medical problem. In America, the national average for C-section rates are almost eight times greater than in Europe. Melissa's ob-gyn visits are held in windowless, institutional-feeling rooms. Once, when Melissa asked about a pregnancy tea she was considering taking, the doctor rolled her eyes: "Doesn't do anything," she said. "Take as much as you want, or don't."

Now, while waiting for the subway in a dank post-Sandy station, Melissa says: "That's the way they think: if it's not Western medicine, they write it off completely."

We've begun researching alternatives, but the only birthing center we can find is an hour away in Brooklyn, and we hear it might be closing. We have already considered and rejected home birth. "Imagine a water birth in our fish tank of a bathtub!" Melissa says. "I don't even fit in it." For now, we stick with the hospital.

As we wait for the train, I realize this is my first time in the subway since Sandy. On the opposite track, a mucky train pulls up, looking like it slithered out of a swamp. Trash overflows the bins and is scattered throughout the platform. The wet station feels pre-apocalyptic.

BARELY A WEEK AFTER the most damaging storm in New York's history, another big one is racing toward us, this time a nor'easter.

"I just can't get used to this new weather," the cashier at Amy's Bread says, as she rings up my coffee and half baguette. She sighs. "But I guess I will. People always get used to things."

I take my breakfast to a table by the window and sit. The radio is on. Everybody listens to the minute-by-minute report of the approaching nor'easter. They're saying it won't be another Sandy. But after the trauma of what just happened, Amy's customers nevertheless snatch up multiple loaves of bread, then rush to hole up in apartments. The wind picks up outside, and a medium-sized tree branch snaps off and slaps against Amy's window. Pedestrians stride by, clutching scarves. *People always get used to things.* That's a *Homo sapiens* specialty: get used to things, adapt, be resilient. This ability turned us — Jared Diamond's once little-noteworthy "third chimpanzee" — into Earth's dominant species, a species now numbering seven billion and counting. In fact, a growing number of scientists now call our geological era the Anthropocene, after the primate that has so fundamentally changed the Earth.

I finish breakfast and step out into the blustery winds of Bleecker Street. The radio says the worst part of the storm is about an hour off. I should seek shelter in the apartment, hunker down.

Instead, I impulsively bypass Cornelia, walking Morton across Seventh Avenue, and drop down to Pier 45. It's 10:35 AM per the old Lackawanna clock tower across the Hudson in Hoboken, a city that still has thirty thousand homeless people from Sandy. I'm the only one on the pier.

Soon a mist of drizzle blows over, coating my face. Then the wind increases, blowing past the Freedom Tower and disappearing into gray clouds. When the sprinkle turns to big raindrops, it's time for me to flee. Just last week, after all, Pier 45 was underwater. Many New Yorkers died. Still, I want to meet the storm.

The downpour hits. Through Pier 45's little strip of grass I run, whooping and kicking up water, alone on a Manhattan pier. Three seagulls take flight from the handrail, braving the weather. One of them dives into the water, snatching out a silvery fish! Another of the gulls, envious of the catch, chases after the one with the flapping fish in its beak. When they cross the pier, I chase them both, squawking as loud as I can, but they don't notice, my calls lost in the storm. I jog back to the apartment.

Soaked and shivering, I arrive to the hiss of our half-century-old heater. I light a fire with branches from Tar Beach. Then it starts snowing. Snow in November? The flakes fall onto the brick-red fire escapes. Thick steam-clouds billow from the neighboring building's heating system, and I hear the whine of a band saw as a new building goes up. They're filling a lovely courtyard below with yet another building, working even in this nor'easter. When I asked about it the other day, they told me they hold a permit for the two-year project. *Noise.* Every weekday from eight to five in our micro and on Tar Beach... for the next two years.

I've really been feeling the blues the past few days. It's more than Sandy alone, more than the typical ups and downs of life. I know that so much is so very good. Squeaker is healthy. We'll soon see Amaya — Melissa's been saving up her vacation leave and we'll be taking a big trip to visit her in Bolivia. And I'm living Slow — finding, in Manhattan, what nature writer John Hay calls "the elemental life," beyond air-treated, fluorescent-lit human boxes. I feel the city's wind and water, my sweat and shivers. I feel the elation of meeting the storm on Pier 45. Wind gusts through my lungs, rushes out in cries to seagulls; our tiny apartment grows a pyramid of skylights to the great gray vault of sky now angrily snowing over the Statue of Liberty, the Verrazano Bridge.

The storm is inside. I get up, go into the kitchen, and open a bottle of wine. It's barely noon, but I feel unsteady. I drink the first glass quickly, then pour more. The snow thrashes around outside, the windows frost over. A side of me knows that humans either will or will not make it through climate change, through the insidious Indian Head alarms — the drones and nukes and biological weapons. Humans will or will not make it through biodiversity loss, through exhausting population growth and rising per-capita consumption. Perhaps, like Bloomberg's global warming epiphany, we'll even seize disaster as a chance to change. Perhaps. But still, on a daily basis, when I see the hollow exercise of voting, see the ways so many around me fill their days and their lives, see how heavily conditioned we are by advertising and marketing and family pressures — springing from a powerful, ecocidal culture with an imperative to grow — it feels oppressive. Not hopeless, but unwelcoming to me.

A WOMAN LIVING TWO BUILDINGS UP from us on Cornelia is raped.

It happened at 2 AM the previous night, the night after the storm. The guy was hiding in the building's courtyard; he raped her there. My building neighbors plaster signs about it in our stairwell, by the mailboxes. On the gate of our horse entrance, the hand-lettered sign reads: "PULL the gate CLOSED so it latches!" Below it, the time and place of the rape. Nobody has been apprehended.

It could have been Melissa, I think when I hear about it, fists clenched. It could have been my pregnant wife.

The evening after the rape, Melissa is below — safe — in the apartment as I, having fully abandoned my "ghost pregnancy," drink a lot of red wine alone atop Tar Beach. No more firewood up here — Sandy reduced our tree canopy by half, leaving hardly a branch for the nor'easter to topple — and all I can picture is that angry man, ripping off her skirt, violating her. First, the Cornelia Street crack dealer, now the Cornelia Street rapist. They're drilling below me, inside the rising new building, working at night, too, shattering even the half-moon peace of the Beach.

I finish the bottle. It's dark and cold. My mind goes to the place it does at the darkest moments. Civil War Liberia, where rape was so common that most women I knew admitted to always wearing tight shorts under their jeans or skirts — a near-useless barrier to rape, but all they had. I feel for those women. Feel for our neighbor.

Violence. I scratch at a wound, a memory I'm always suppressing, one worse than hunkering down in Buchanan with what might have been my last plate of palm butter.

It happened even farther inside the jungle. Twelve hours from the capital, outside of Greenville, crossing a checkpoint. A teenage soldier defending the border of a foreign timber concession.

"Get down!" he yells at me. Amphetamine strips on his face. AK-47.

I shake my head. I'm sitting shotgun next to Momo, my driver. Momo pleads with him, half in a whisper: "But, *boss.* Whiteman bringing food to the refugees-o! Let us pass, I beg you."

The soldier is drugged. He's still staring at me. Commanders feed the kids amphetamines through cuts on their faces to keep them primed for fighting. Keep them a little crazy. Crazy enough to defend a Malaysian logging company clear-cutting an ancient rainforest so the wood can be shipped to Chinese coastal factories, where it's made into cheap furniture sold by Walmart in Ohio.

"Get DOWN!" he repeats, even louder.

I look out the truck window, down into the ditch beside the road. The ditch looks like an open grave. If I get down, this is where I'll die. Again, I shake my head.

He yanks open my door. Nods for me to step down.

I sweat in the tropical evening, something thick and ugly caught in my throat. *I'm going to die here. Outside Greenville, in a ditch, on the edge of a timber concession. Die, on a foul frontline of globalization.*

Momo, just in time, fishes out a wad of green-and-red Liberty notes and holds the Christmas-colored currency out to the boy.

He looks at it. Looks at me. Looks at it again. Then he seizes the Liberty, kicks my door shut, and drops the check-point rope.

Because of Momo's Liberty, I don't die. But looking in the rearview mirror as we bounce away down the dirt road, driving toward the internally displaced people we're to feed, I know that part of my innocence does. That's because that boy with the drug strips on his face is already dead on that foul frontline of globalization. No amount of Liberty is going to save him.

THE NEXT MORNING, HUNGOVER, I take the subway to the Bronx Zoo. I spend hours with chimpanzees, elephants, tigers, macaws. With nonrapists, non–drone killers, non–climate changers. I'm sick of my species, sick of myself. On the way out of the zoo, I find a secluded stretch of woods, strip to my boxers, and leap into a small river, a tributary I've come to call the Bronx River, which dumps into the Hudson on its journey south.

I sink. Sink toward the bottom. Cannonball to the icy, muddy floor. It's probably polluted. There are surely broken bottles down here, maybe medical waste, syringes. I don't care. I want to kill some memories and feelings.

I know I'm unwell. This is worse than planes over Queens, worse than workaholism, even, somehow, worse than Rachel Wetzsteon and five stories down from Tar Beach. It's a planet with drug strips on its face, a planet with AKs in the hands of child soldiers, a planet fumed up by too many cars and industrial plants. A planet of Frankenstorms.

Down on the bottom of the river it's freezing, silent. After some seconds, the cold doesn't sting. My head tumbles forward and touches mud. The peace down there. Womb-time. No mind time.

No rape time. No kid-soldier time. No suicide time. No Sandy time.

Oxygen expiring, I unfurl from my tight ball and shoot, spring-like, to the airy surface. I draw breath, exhale, and sink back into muddy silence.

On the subway back home, my hair still wet from the river, I wonder if I'm depressed. *I'm unwell*, I think, *but also feral and free*. But that's crazy talk, right? I study the people beside me on the train. They exude workday exhaustion. Mopping Wall Street floors, assisting a dentist, cooking in a smoky kitchen. The "lucky" ones get to prepare legal briefs and fill cavities, but they too look spent. I hear macaw cries, the cry of a baby chimpanzee; I feel the scales of fish around me in the river and sink into silence. I'm unwell, but also feral and free.

Is it depression that makes me want to merge with every natural feature of the city I see, even a river in cold November? Chellis Glendinning, in her book *My Name Is Chellis and I'm in Recovery from Western Civilization,* talks about how mental illness is often related to modern humanity's great divorce from nature. I've opened myself up to the pain of that divorce all the more by going Slow. At the bottom of the Bronx River, I feel no pain.

SILENCE.

It slips into me after the Bronx. I talk less and less in the following days.

When I receive an email invitation to speak — at the Fez Forum on the Alliance of Civilizations, in Morocco — I can't imagine accepting. Burn all that carbon to get me to North Africa...to *speak?* Dress up and lecture from a podium? All I want to do is be mute.

There are psychologists in New York who specifically attend to former aid workers. People who served in places like Liberia. A side of me wonders if I need to visit one, and another side of me feels like healing is a matter of allowing the space for things to come back into alignment. *Space.* The Rambles. Pier 45. The third story. A Harriman lean-to. Silence is part of allowing the space to realign. I've got this psychic garbage in me, the kind all of us have, so how do I let it go?

Melissa and I, after Amanbir's Golden Bridge kundalini class, eat a silent meal at Back Forty West, an organic locavore bistro in SoHo. Aside from ordering, we spend two and a half hours in silence. Every table around us turns over, folks rushing to the bar or the theater, as the sky through the window drains of light like a squid releasing each drop of its ink.

Tastes and textures cross our lips as we tent hands across the table. I notice the paintings and photos all clumped together — a good hundred of them — on one single side of the room. The opposite wall is totally blank, Cornelia-micro blank, with nothing more than two soft-lit lamps. Everything on one side, nothing on the other. My eyes travel over the waxy surface of the candle flickering between us in a thin crystal cup and come to rest on a bone.

A cow's large thighbone, dried and white, on an otherwise empty side table, a parched white beauty-mark amid the dozens of animate *Homo sapiens*, their taut skins holding back blood, plasma, living bone and marrow. Melissa is a little pinker than before, her gaze lying just beyond the candle on my empty plate. When I retake her hand, I see her eyes are moist. I give her a questioning glance. She shakes her head, smiles. She knows I am hurting inside. She knows she can't touch that hurt, but she sees it echoing inside me. While I find solace in silence, the extrovert in her yearns to talk. I start to speak, but she reaches out a knowing finger and presses it to my lips.

PART 3

WINTER TO SPRING
Flight Paths

13. SLOW TRAVEL

IN FEZ, MOROCCO, I BREAK MY SILENCE.

"I know what global warming feels like," I tell an audience of hundreds sitting beneath the vaulted ceiling of the Arabesque conference room. Delegates from some forty countries are here, along with the local youth so pivotal in the Arab Spring, which started here in Morocco.

I speak. I speak about the flood, the carnage, the billions in destruction, the absence of public transport, electricity. I had always known the facts on climate change and had spoken to groups passionately about its impact. But I'd never been able to talk about how it affected me in a tangible way — how those numbers translated in terms of human lives. In terms of the home my neighbors and I have made on our little piece of E*air*th. Faces — Arab and Asian, African and European — open faces, listening ones. Most people wear headphones for interpretation into Arabic, French, and Chinese. Through the gauze of a slight delay, I watch people's body language when they capture what this New Yorker is telling them: one of the world's richest cities was brought to its knees by climate change.

When I finish, I feel a buoyancy to my spirit for the first time in a long while. I rise, a little, from where I had cannon-balled to the river bottom.

And I continue to rise, ever so subtly, during four intense days at the Fez Forum, a Third World–organized quasi-UN, without the rules and hierarchy. Yes, we dress in suits and sit through long proceedings and working lunches. But the forum is alive, perhaps seeded with an Arab Spring–inspired spirit that we actually *can* confront the world's problems, all of them at once, and together.

"Without test, there is no testimony," an East African delegate says to me, perhaps reading between the lines of my speech, intuiting the way, in Fez, I'm letting go of some of the psychic garbage that weighed me down on the wrecked Pier 45, in the flooded subway tunnels, in the polluted Bronx River. I listen, letting more of the garbage go. I listen to a Filipino congresswoman with a novel take on gender equality in government. I listen to a bubbling sociology professor from Istanbul who wants to bridge his country to both the Arab world and the West. I listen to Moroccan university students telling me about their ongoing struggles.

I also speak. About Sandy, about healing culture and economy, aligning with a finite Earth. I don't have to be fearfully mute. The Moroccan government has brought me in. I'm given a platform; I *use* it, paying close attention to that delicate balance between listening and speaking — some statistics here, an affirmation there, lots of smiles and humor to break down barriers of superficial difference. I realize that, inspired by the giving and hopeful world delegates around me, I'm breaking through the shell I had built around myself in New York. I'm finding ways to connect and share with others, but perhaps most importantly — to serve. By the fourth day of the Fez Forum, the place ignites with a kind of Burning Man energy that's directed to a final statement of how we can "ally civilizations" to get beyond environmental destruction, war, and the myriad forms of oppression through education campaigns and smarter policies. We, the world's diverse array of people, here in Morocco, have a say in the paradigm.

By forum's end, I'm utterly exhausted, but I am no longer at river's bottom. Though still underwater, I have floated halfway toward the surface. Hugging new friends good-bye as they head to the Casablanca airport to return to their busy work schedules, I decide to do something different. I've already burned the carbon to get here — and have flexibility with the NYU semester finished and Melissa working late every day in advance of our Bolivia trip — so I decide to stay in Morocco for ten more days, experimenting with another branch of the global Slow phenomenon: something called Slow Travel.

I ONCE HEARD A UNITARIAN MINISTER SAY: "Blessed are those who don't know where they are going after service today." After the Fez Forum, I don't know where I'm going. I hop the next bus leaving the city's main terminal, riding it through the parched Atlas Mountains to Morocco's Berber capital, Azrou, three hours south of Fez.

It turns out Azrou isn't a tourist destination. The 100,000-inhabitant town is gritty and mountainous and cold. Hardly anyone speaks Arabic, let alone French. Communicating through gestures, I make my way up winding roads to the Panorama Hotel, where, exhausted from Fez, I happily lie around the lounge, eating vegetable *tagine* over couscous and sipping mint tea. I get to know the hotel staff — there are few guests — with whom I communicate through our combined smatterings of English and French.

A day passes, then two. It's freeing to have no plan. I stick around the Panorama lobby, enjoying the smiles and drinking mint tea with the twenty-six-year-old Melina, a hotel receptionist with sing-song French and almond-shaped eyes. Her rather timeless attitude sucks me in and really captures what Slow Travel is: absorption. It's not about collecting points on an itinerary to match a string of digital photos, the way one might overstuff a home with knickknacks. As one Slow Traveler put it to me, "It's about the quality of attention you bring into a place."

The only outing I take in Azrou is made in homage of my non–*Homo sapien* side. Just as the chimpanzees and elephants of the Bronx Zoo breathed life back into my psyche, I'm drawn to visit the wild but friendly tribe of apes in the mountains just above Azrou. I take a *grand taxi* — the decades-old, shared-ride Mercedes cars that serve out-of-city destinations throughout Morocco — up the winding road to the forest. Snow begins to fall, and I start to make out the shapes of these furry creatures. A bit surreal, the weather makes me think of the snowflakes that blanketed my own inner storm just a few weeks back. Getting out of the taxi, I'm amazed that the apes are already so close — a mother, a father, and a little baby ape hastily climb a nearby tree.

The next morning I ride another bus eight hours west,

along the country's Atlas Mountain spine, to lively Marrakech. On my second day there, I visit the striking adobe remains of the sixteenth-century El Badi Palace, an urban sanctuary. I feel my footfalls as I move, snail-paced, through the chambers of Saadian princes who once came here to visit Sultan Ahmad al-Mansur.

El Badi means "the marvel," once one of the world's most remarkable monuments. As I slow walk, my imagination tumbles through the ages — the Mansurian Dynasty built the palace after driving out the Christians, proclaiming themselves Muhammad's direct descendants, and declaring Marrakech their sultanate. Then, Sultan al-Mansur constructed this marvel in the late sixteenth century while simultaneously conquering the West African Songhai Empire and leading a gold rush to the Niger River. I'm moved by the transience of al-Mansur's vision, his kingdom falling into anarchy before he died. Eventually, Moulay al-Rashid captured Marrakech in 1669 and sacked El Badi, moving much of its building materials to Meknes, leaving behind, eventually, this silent ruin.

Enough facts. Slow Travel is not just learning about a destination but feeling it, slipping into the senses. As I step into the warm sunlight of a palace courtyard the size of a few football fields, a red veneer floats above four orange groves, the trees so bright with their fruits that they almost look artificial. I pick and eat one, anything but artificial. I come upon the palace olive grove and pick an olive — this fruit unripe, a stone rolling across the inside of my hand. I look up at the dozen storks in arch, black-and-white attention above me. A mere twenty or so tourists are in the entire place, and I feel the space and silence around me.

Two hours pass. Then three. Sultan al-Mansur is gone. Moulay al-Rashid is gone. With me now, in this marvel, awe. A call to prayer echoes from the surrounding mosques beyond the orange and olive groves. Across the terrace, several people bow toward Mecca, and from the terrace, I look out over a Marrakech skyline, noticing that, unlike the city I inhabit, the highest buildings here aren't Citibank, Chrysler, and Bank of America. They are the spires of mosques. God — the present moment, the *hours*, the angelus — rises higher than the strongholds of profit and exchange.

"SKIP EL BADI PALACE," an early-thirties Canadian tourist, Jane, tells me over breakfast the next morning, at the *riad* — the Moroccan-style B&B — where we're both staying. "Fifteen minutes was enough for us. Who needs more old adobe?"

Her husband, Kyle, looks up from his smartphone. "Marrakech is really just a tourist trap," he says, then he tells Jane about an email from a friend going to the wedding they'll be attending in Toronto this weekend.

Jane pulls her phone out, too, and they discuss other social media updates, seeming to neither taste the *khobz* bread and strong Moroccan coffee nor enjoy our rooftop view.

Jane finally puts down the gadget, sighs loudly as if exhaling stress. "We fly back to Toronto tonight, just for the wedding, and then it's South America for five weeks. There's so much to see."

Kyle frowns over his phone, tapping it. Jane goes on: "We need to cover all of South America in just five weeks. What I need is just a week to settle somewhere to catch my breath!" It turns out they are on a four-month extended honeymoon.

"Since then it's probably kids and mortgages and three weeks a year off," Jane says, "we need to squeeze as much out of it as we can." Kyle continues to tap, and she talks and talks till I'm dizzy — the itinerary points she's collected so far (Thailand, Australia, Tunisia) swerving in and out of the upcoming South American destinations (Rio, Salvador, Buenos Aires). "It's not enough time to do the whole world," Jane finally says.

Kyle's face snaps up. "Can you believe the shit Jeff posts on Facebook? Check this out..."

I finish breakfast and walk to a secluded nook on the *riad* roof. Gazing over the *souk* market and mosque spires, I realize I used to be Jane and Kyle. At nineteen, I and my best friend, Alex, hit nineteen European countries in two months on our Eurail passes, with the goal of hacky-sacking in front of every famous monument on the continent. We had passersby snap photos of us doing stalls and kicking "rainbows" in front of the Eiffel Tower, the Berlin Wall, the Leaning Tower of Pisa. I was my fellow delegates at the Fez Forum as well, attending conferences and immediately thereafter jetting to another work commitment, knowing nothing about the places I was in.

A quiet hour passes. I think on New York and the friends who have passed through our Slow Year on visits to and through our oft-transited city. One married couple, high school friends of Melissa's, now have two small children and lucrative finance jobs in Rome; they met us for dinner in the West Village. They downed mixed drinks, harried from their fast-paced weeklong escape from their jobs. They had only one day in New York before hitting Los Angeles (his parents), Chicago (hers), and then back to Rome. All those airports, and with two children!

How can it be, I wonder, breathing the sweet scent coming

from the tangerine trees on the rooftop, that the most successful among Rich World professionals often seem the most enslaved? Over and over I see in my own tribe — in the very folks who advertisements say the world should aspire to emulate — the most scattered energies, the thinnest smiles. It strikes me, on Tar Beach Marrakech, that it's precisely the wealthiest and most successful who are the most shaped into Analytical Life. That's what delivers their success, and it's also what tears them out of the aliveness of their bodies, out of the sensuous present.

"I LOVE THE ROMANTIC POETS. Do you?"

I turn around. Beside the tangerine tree, it's Karim. We've been chatting on and off through my several days here at the Marrakech *riad*, where the thin, bright-eyed twenty-five-year-old works. I ask Karim what he means.

"The Lebanese Kahlil Gibran. Or your Thoreau! Romantic poets go away from civilization to small villages, to isolated places, to just be with the flowers and the birds and the rivers, and to write poetry about them. But they rarely become well-known because they are too far from the cities."

He looks down into the car-free streets of the medieval quarter below us and says: "But there's no money in romantic poetry. I tried it for a while, but you have to live a very poor life, and you have nothing for your marriage." Karim is from a small Moroccan village and says he came to Marrakech to study English literature and work. The only job he could find was in this hotel.

Like many Moroccans I've been meeting, Karim exudes an air of having all the time in the world. A warm, genuine smile never seems to leave his face; in my life, I've seen this kind of uninhibited joy in greater abundance the lower a country's GDP (in "poorer" countries, as some might dub them). As we talk on the *riad* roof, I find Karim embodies the tension that most people feel between nature and civilization — between, on the one hand, wanting to be a free creature and, on the other, wanting to belong to society. I ask him why he doesn't work for a few years in Marrakech, save money, and thereby have the means to become a "romantic poet," or at least move back to the countryside, marry, and live a more peaceful life closer to nature.

"Even if I were to work so hard for three, four, five years, I would never save money! This job...they don't pay us." He describes how King Mohammed VI, Morocco's head of state, controls billions of dollars and palaces all over the country and how the democratic movements have gained little in the Arab Spring. Karim wants something to change so he can, as he puts it, "become free." This is the precise tension in the Leisure Ethic that is so often misunderstood: it cures affluenza, not poverty and inequality. Then again, more of the same — more consumption, gadgetry, and speed, the conventional recipe for development — doesn't cure poverty and inequality either. The cure for this is another paradigm.

Calls to prayer sound from below. Karim's face lights up. "Excuse me," he says, "it's time to go. I must pray."

AS DAYS PASS, I keep traveling, intuition as guide, until the cramped, shared *grand taxi* I'm in rolls into the coastal city of Agadir.

Agadir is Morocco's Miami — flashy and high-rolling — and as I check into one of its cheaper, on-the-surface cheesy resort hotels, I wonder if my intuition is on the fritz if it landed me in this town.

"Cheap," in this case, merely means its sixties décor hasn't been updated, but the place is clean and has a pool, and it's filled with hundreds of German tourists. All of the signs, menus, and information packets are *auf Deutsch*. I speak German with folks in the lobby and at breakfast the next morning. It's refreshing to connect with others in a language that is not your own. Memories of my studies in East Germany flood in. They say that with each language you have a slightly different personality. In Agadir I explore my German self, the cadence of my words a different tenor. It's another aspect of Slow Travel: flowing freely with whatever the road brings your way.

In that light-hearted spirit, that evening I think: *Why not put on my suit?* It's been folded at the bottom of my backpack since the conference in Fez. I pull it out — not too wrinkled. Feeling a little formal, I strut the boardwalk in my suit, enjoying a Slow walk alongside locals and foreigners, then I savor a fish dinner in Leblanc, overlooking the water. I blend. Traveling, nobody has any preconceptions about you, allowing you to play.

The next day, I awake to incongruity: sitting on an old waterbed in a dated Agadir resort, sunlight streaming in to my third-floor room, a highway rushing by beyond the swimming pool. I luxuriate in the sunlight, in the room's frayed interior, in the smell of sea air, in the German still buzzing in my head. The texture of this moment is completely different from anything I've experienced in my life. When have I been in the north of Africa, thinking in German, smelling the ocean, hearing a freeway? Something extraordinary in this elicits joy.

Korean is filled w/nuance respect for status, Confucian ethics/thinking in the language dreaming in the language

The slow pacing allows for integrating the experience into your DNA — to incubate creativity need time for the experience to connect in the brain — Krista Tippet Creativity podcast

It's similar to the mystical feeling I had in the El Badi Palace in Marrakech, a recurring experience throughout the trip. I've been centered in the present moment and focused almost solely on connecting with the people and places I encounter. Rather than seek a particular experience, I accept whatever I find and suddenly realize that it's precisely what's *not* special about this moment — overlooking a highway in the morning sunlight — that's special. It's unstandard, unbranded, undefined, and ephemeral. In the West, we market experiences like commodities; uniqueness and texture are nearly always a market niche. We think America encourages and allows for every type of style and taste, but commerce defines our style, our taste, our experience, and we are encouraged to keep buying that uniqueness again and again. I may love a certain type of video game, or mountain biking or paragliding, or I may prefer Goth style or ping pong or a type of literature or Middle Eastern lounge music — whatever — but at root this has already been commodified into a niche, this desire has been socialized into me. Who have *I* been in my Slow Year? Prodigy Coffee, Golden Bridge Yoga, Pearl scallops, each of them, on one level, a commodity out of which I build an identity.

The only thing that defines this moment in Agadir is my experience of it. It embodies a way of living in which every moment reinvents everything. It's the flaneur sensibility I've tried to cultivate, and I see it's now in my travel DNA. Every moment incubates creativity. This feeling of timelessness and texture, elation and groundedness, defies commodification, has no market niche. As silly as it was to dress in a suit and go to a restaurant last night, it felt equally wonderful. So did scrunching, with six others, into a 1960s Mercedes *grand taxi* all day yesterday, literally leaning

who are you from your passions/preferences your identity

forward onto my knees for hours on end, sandwiched between several Moroccans, terrible music blaring on the tinny stereo, the smell of sweat mixing with the traffic fumes.

This sensibility is one I've seen in indigenous cultures around the world, and I'm finding it in pockets of Slow Living in New York City. Now, traveling in Morocco, I feel like there's nothing greater in life that I could discover than this. It's beyond ideology, politics, or anything that could be put into language. It is being present — fully present — in the moment, thereby allowing to flourish the extreme freedom of our creaturedom, which is far beyond society, the media, globalization, or anything else. More to the point, there is no reason this extreme freedom can't be brought into the heart of the busiest city on Earth. I've already located a few of those nonmonetized corners: Pier 45 idling, Rockaway waves, Tar Beach dovewatching, the Central Park Ramble. And while we're creating urban joy and centeredness for ourselves, we're also a spark that can reshape society.

MY TRIP IS ALMOST OVER. From my structured visit to Fez to the free-flowing moments in Azrou, Marrakech, and Agadir, I feel full. The gold coins are once again overflowing. I feel a tug to return home to New York. Yet, as Martin Buber says, "Every journey has a secret destination, of which the traveler is unaware." I'm about to discover that this trip, which has become my pilgrimage, holds its own secret destination.

I'm sweaty and covered in Saharan dust at the *grand taxi* station behind the *souk* in Agadir. I want to go to Essaouira, about three hours away, where I'll catch my plane back to JFK in a few days.

I stand around for a half hour. I'm the only passenger for Essaouira, when finally a man in his late thirties — black leather jacket, handsome mustache, black hair trimmed short in a Western style, dark eyes — offers to take me right now for twenty dollars. It seems like a deal. The going price is ten dollars for each person in a full taxi — but filling a *grand taxi* with five more Essaouira-bound travelers could take hours. So I agree.

The taxi driver says he's Rashid and mentions in his deep-cadenced French that, *s'il vous plaît*, we'll be filling a few more of the seats right outside town. Of course, no problem.

The Atlantic opens in bright blue as we take the curves, fast, out of Agadir, crossing a mountain into the next village. There, the real fun starts.

My twenty dollars has reserved me the two seats up front, but Rashid makes sure to fill up the four spots in back as often as he can. We stop for not just the few passengers I was imagining, but rather for some thirty altogether! Rashid takes them on short routes, nobody going even half the distance to Essaouira. Always beaming, he loads parcels into the trunk, gives change, chats pleasantly with each passenger. At one point we stop for three six-foot Bedouin traders who pack their stuff into the trunk around my backpack as best they can, then squeeze into the back seat. When I attempt to offer the space beside me up front, Rashid vehemently disallows it. One of the Bedouins, for the twenty minutes he's with us, talks nonstop in the loudest, harshest Arabic voice I've heard on the trip. We drop the traders off in what seems like an uninhabited stretch of desert, and then Rashid motors on, quickly filling up the taxi with more passengers.

Fully transformed by my Agadir experience, I savor how my presumed express taxi turns into a local. At various stops, I get out, stretch, and inhale the local scent shed. I buy a guava juice in one hamlet, sipping it slowly as we cross the mountains, its sugars substituting for my usual afternoon coffee. Rashid turns out to be a gentleman, speaks in smooth French, and listens attentively to every sentence I utter, answering respectfully. He picks up anyone, regardless of how rich or poor they look. At one point, he sees, too late, an old woman in tattered clothes and burka on the side of the road, so he pulls his *grand taxi* over, hits reverse, and backs up twenty yards to pick her up — then refuses her two *dirham* fare at the end. Honking and smiling at friends in each village we pass, he tells me he's driven the Agadir-Essaouira route "a thousand times, and still I love it."

When we arrive in Essaouira, Rashid asks me where I'm staying. When I say I don't have a hotel yet, he insists I stay with his family.

"Thank you, Rashid, but I'll find a place."

He sounds disappointed but doesn't press me. He offers me an alternative: he'll show me a simple and inexpensive hotel near his home, and I can join his family for a meal the day before I leave.

We motor through the Essaouira outskirts to the edge of its gorgeous white-walled old city, the medina. After parking, we walk through the city walls toward Rashid's neighborhood, which he says is right inside the medina, and I feel the calm of the Atlantic-washed vibe, the smell of salt water mixed with a little sweat and urine, the vault of baby-blue sky above laced with mauve from the setting sun. I also feel a bit nervous

— Rashid's is a humble neighborhood, and it will soon be dark. We are warned in the West that terrorists spring from Arab neighborhoods like this, and Rashid's a stranger.

My worry melts away when he shows me the building where he lives and points across the way to a small hotel with a welcoming, simple entrance. From the small balcony above where we stand, a squeal of delight cuts the evening calm: Rashid's youngest child calls out to his father, welcoming him home.

I LOVE ESSAOUIRA. The constantly blue sky, its salty-scented warmth, and the ten thousand seagulls perching on every roof and waking me up from their perches in the mornings. There's so much to do here — surf, eat in sea-facing restaurants, receive argon oil massages, shop in the medina's markets — but I do none of them. I sleep soundly in the simple hotel room. It's enough to just be here within the walls of the old city, to listen to the birds, to look at the rainbow-colored laundry hanging from people's roofs, and to know that not far away are Rashid and his family, living their daily lives here in the medina as I do mine in the West Village.

I yearn to do my own laundry. There's something incredibly pleasant about doing your own laundry while traveling instead of paying someone to do it. I simply throw my clothes into the shower, pour on a bit of shampoo, stomp them with my feet as I bathe, wring them out, and hang them on the roof, clandestinely, alongside the hotel's guest sheets and towels. An hour later they're almost dry, and the physical work of wringing out clothes and hanging them becomes a meditation, an act of regular daily living on a rooftop half a world from home.

On my final day, I meet Rashid just outside his building to join his family for a midday meal. We climb the five small flights of stairs, and I sense a strange familiarity. He opens the door and invites me in, smiling proudly as though ushering me into his palace.

I have a through-the-looking-glass feeling when I step inside: one bedroom, an only-room. A tiny kitchen, a bathroom you have to squeeze into. About 450 square feet. I've come all the way to Essaouira, Morocco, and found our Cornelia Street micro-apartment.

Instead of two, five souls live here. Rashid, his smiling wife, Suzette, who is preparing our meal, and three young kids, the smallest of whom, three-year-old Hadisha, runs up and hugs my leg to welcome me.

We eat our *tagine* slowly. I taste the complexity of the spices, a tapestry of delight wrapping around my tongue, delving into taste buds I never knew I had, even beyond those awakened by the gourmet meals Melissa and I sought out in the West Village. As we eat, Rashid tells stories and asks about my travels. They are particularly amused when I mention how much I enjoyed the hotel's rooftop view of the medina while washing my clothes. A foreigner, a man, doing his own laundry on a rooftop in their neighborhood — what a surprise! Suzette jokes that I'm welcome to take down their laundry from their rooftop if I love the view so much.

I insist on just that. Despite Rashid's refusal, I make my way up to the roof, the children on my heels.

I take down their laundry. When it's all down, I fold clothes with the whole family, Rashid included, the black shadows of seagulls on the white wall behind the kids, the ocean beyond like a royal blue Persian rug, two parakeet cages full of birdsong. I'm happy. It strikes me that the grand theories that attempt to encapsulate the twenty-first century — from Barber's "Jihad vs. McWorld" to Fukuyama's end of history — carry partial truths but miss the much subtler core pivot of our era. Our planet, our happiness, and our children's future depend upon finding equilibrium through cultivating the still, the small, the Slow.

[handwritten margin notes:]

introduce more silence -

reason for silence to listen to the still small voice w/in

what we know the still small voice within

Cultivating the still/ moving, pulsating changing energy of the universe + so we still ourselves so we can feel it/sense it before joining it again

order as gift

14. NEWYORQUINOS

RETURNING HOME from Morocco, I hear New York afresh. It's almost Christmas, and bells ring through Manhattan. Pompeii Church's bells, heard from an ice-slicked Tar Beach. Salvation Army Santa bells at the West 4th Street subway entrance. Bells on a golden retriever walking past the giant twinkling Christmas tree under the Washington Square Arch. The city's bells summon me to presence, just as the calls to prayer did in Morocco, sounding from the mosques of Marrakech, Azrou, Fez. My mother sends me, for Christmas, a book that immediately accompanies me everywhere, Macrina Wiederkehr's *Seven Sacred Pauses*, an ecumenical guide to the Benedictine "hours" — calls to mindfulness at seven points during the day and night. I dog-ear the book, its meditations deepening the wintry sunrises, midmornings, noon...and the nighttime's Great Silence.

Melissa's parents pay a holiday visit to New York from

[handwritten margin notes: "how many times do Muslims pray - 5 why 7?"]

Santa Fe. Since they're Episcopalians, we take them to high mass at St. Luke's Cathedral around the block. It's the first time I've entered the neo-Gothic structure beside St. Luke's oft-trod gardens on Greenwich Street, a favorite urban sanctuary. Dressed in medieval-looking garments, a procession of ministers, deacons, and acolytes stride by, burning strong, thick incense, and my body vibrates with the thundering organ. Another day, Melissa and I follow the peal of bells to the "Jazz Mass" at the Christopher Street Methodist church around the block. There, a polished jazz quartet improvs through the service, and in a "communal sermon," the minister walks the aisles questioning.

Today's theme: *Can I forgive myself?*

It was in Morocco, it strikes me, as I sit during a bright clarinet solo at the end of the Jazz Mass, that I dropped something dense. A load of frustration and guilt, a load of past. Befriending a romantic poet, collecting laundry from an Essaouira rooftop — touching a Slower culture — I dropped the weight of feeling persecuted by the existence of child soldiers, Frankenstorms, and ecocide. I now feel lighter in spirit than I ever have in Manhattan. I've come up from the mud at river bottom, cracked the sunny surface, and now take flight, touching down at will into the river's translucence. Like never before, I appreciate water.

Wandering the Village, I break off icicles of all sizes — frozen daggers from drainpipes, iridescent nodules on pine needles — and let them melt on my skin and gums. On Tar Beach, I catch snowflakes on my tongue, a practice I learned from my first-grade teacher, Mrs. Meyers, who, when it would start to snow, would stop whatever we were doing and usher the entire class outside. "Open your mouths!" she'd cry. "One snowflake each and then back inside!" Running out into the flakes, I'd present my pink tongue to the heavens.

Steam, too. After plough-pose in our fish-tank tub, I watch the mirror fog, watch our bedroom cube cloud when I open the door. Drying off, unhurriedly, my skin relishes the boundary between wet and dry. One evening, I leave my body a little moist and, wrapped in a towel, sit beside Melissa on our only-room daybed. The fire blazing, I sense the dampness evaporate as we hold hands and sip tea. The fire yawns to embers, and snowmelt drips down the chimney and sizzles in the orange coals. We're content. I remember something, from a hot day in August, a surprise thunderstorm that caught us on Pier 45. Instead of running for shelter, we drank from the sky, kicked puddles, sat down in an erstwhile tributary draining from the bike path into the Hudson. Teeth chattering, we ran back to the micro to towel each other off.

"What are you thinking?" I ask Melissa, snowmelt still dripping into the fireplace, sizzling.

She gets up and puts a log on the fire. "About Bolivia," she says, blowing the coals back.

I imagine the frigid Hudson, a few blocks away — flowing always south — toward Amaya. Our long-awaited trip is three days away. "What about Bolivia?"

"It feels like more than a vacation," she says, snuggling once again beside me. "It feels like it could be the end of New York."

We bundle up and head out into the falling snow. In Washington Square Park, a few hundred carolers sing "The Twelve Days of Christmas" under the arch, beside the Christmas tree.

At the periphery, we join the singing for a few bars and then continue on.

Broadway ahead, I hear church bells and I stop. The famous street dazzles with Christmas lights. Still arm-in-arm with Melissa, I realize something's not right. The rush of taxis, shuttling last-minute shoppers. Feathery snowflakes defying Broadway's gravity, dangling in its cheery glow. The steam of Melissa's breath as she huddles close.

What stops me is a memory. A memory of something sublime.

Melissa and me, together, witnessing a wonder. Hundreds of strangers. A fabulous Romanesque arch. A radiant tree, vaulting skyward. *Four calling birds.* A glorious and resonant sound. *Three French Hens.*

A memory, and not even a distant one. It's recent history. Just five minutes back.

We sang a few lines and then scooted, immediately forgetting. *Two turtle doves.*

How intriguing, the forgetting about it! Living in ten-million-inhabitant New York there's always something akin to that spectacle. Someplace small in the world, if three hundred voices would echo like that through a giant arch, it might become legend, passed down for generations. Odes written about it. In gold calligraphy.

But being good New Yorkers, we sang for a sec and split.

Melissa and I backtrack to the arch.

In the square, they're singing "O Holy Night." The arch growing in size, we pass a Salvation Army Santa vigorously ringing her bell, and I'm asking myself, who built that arch? Who assembled the melodious multitudes? How did we *miss* it? Rejoining the group, somebody hands me a copy of the tunes they're caroling. Melissa presses my gloved hand to her expanding womb, and we sing for a good long while.

WE DANCE. To inspire us before our journey to Bolivia tomorrow, Melissa suggests we hit the famous New York salsa club Copacabana.

At Copa, all of *America Latina* spins and gyrates to a dozen-piece salsa orchestra. Cubans and Dominicans, Colombians and Bolivians. We join them on the dance floor. I learned salsa in Guatemala some fifteen years back, and Melissa can also break-on-two.

Out of breath after several songs, we sink into lounge chairs. The orchestra takes a break. We sip — me a mojito and she a juice — and I start telling her about James and Emily. They're a late-twenties British couple I met in Morocco ten days back in the remote oceanfront hamlet of Mirleft at the margins of the Sahara. Two years back, the couple bailed out of secure professional jobs in England, took a risk, and opened a surf school in little Mirleft. It worked. European executives now fly in to learn to surf from James and Emily, and the couple earns enough to rent a modest home on a stark cliff over the Atlantic. They live Slow, shopping for *tagine* veggies at the local *souk*, surfing daily, and listening to Britain's Channel Four streamed through a laptop.

I sip my mojito and add: "I walked the tideline below their house and could see James and Emily on their balcony, overlooking endless water. They're perched on the edge. There's an ocean between them and Britain."

The band is setting up again. Melissa takes my hand. "If

you're not living on the edge, maybe you're taking up too much space." She smiles.

"Slow in New York is about as close to the edge as you can get, without plummeting."

Melissa shrugs. "So I guess the question is what's *our* edge."

I drain my mojito. 1 know she's talking about Bolivia. "I can't imagine leaving New York. We've found a groove."

Then something hits me: My graduate school professor was wrong. *You can't change the culture, Bill. The culture changes* you. By fumbling to live Slow in the world's fastest city, we made a dent. Walking questioning with the NYU students. Giving the Wisdomkeepers the spotlight. Affirming the humanity of Juan the fish-delivery guy and many others. Taking back our time, giving it away. Manhattan changed us, sure; rubbing against its concrete bruises and tenderizes. It's softened our humanity without extracting our souls.

I look out into the club. A hundred *newyorquinos* take to their feet as the band starts up again. Melissa rises, too. She's not too far along in her pregnancy to dance, to board a plane; she wants to salsa, to fly. We approach the dance floor slowly, the sensuous walk of flaneurs. I notice the mix of perfumes, meet others' eyes. Space is tight, but we find our place, and a small space is enough. Melissa sticks her hand out, slightly coquettish, just like little Amaya does whenever we play-dance salsa. My wife and I find our way into the salsa, and I dance with Melissa, Amaya, and belly-baby at the same time.

WE'VE BEEN IN TAMAYSISA (I've changed the name of the actual Bolivian village for privacy's sake) for two weeks when we discover the most beautiful piece of land we've ever seen.

[handwritten margin note:] I love to catch the scent of people as they walk past stealing their essence

Five and a half acres of rolling hillside, creek, and *guaparu* trees bursting with sweet fruit. It's for sale. And nobody else seems to know it is.

We spend hours walking the land, taking in its different angles. "It feels like you're in the countryside," Melissa says, looking out from the property's main hillock, the view overlooking the colonial-style clay *teja* roofs of the 4,000-inhabitant town. "And yet the village square is right there. That's what, a ten-minute stroll?"

Amaya, who now swings from the flowering *tajibo* tree beside us, just announced where the eco-house we envision would be: this knoll, with its 360-degree view encompassing the pueblo, mega-diverse Amboró National Park's buffer zone, and the mountains of Fuerte de Samaipata, a jaguar-shaped Inca ruin.

But local housing prices are rising fast. Others have "discovered" this town; folks from thirty-one countries live here now — folks from Berlin and Paris, Bangkok and Sydney — many of them here to "revillage." Bolivians from the west part of the country, as well as from the nearby city of Santa Cruz, two hours to the east, are finding this an ideal climate. The phenomenon of revillaging is simple: as small towns empty out due to urbanization — that is, cities drawing bodies to urban employers — those small towns have more elbow room and become attractive to urbanites able to de-tether from employers. Take Tamaysisa. Those opening their own business or who, like us, can freelance remotely through the town's high-speed Internet discover a family-friendly community in these cobbled streets as well as a lower cost of living than in cities.

Melissa and I begin negotiations with the property's owner, a businessman from Santa Cruz with a long history in the area.

He's in no rush to sell, and he won't divide it. We make an offer. He counters. It's still too high for us.

Meanwhile, the town increasingly inspires us. Partly due to revillaging, Tamaysisa is home to the meditation retreat Eco-Tao, Brazilian massage, Chinese acupuncture, and even Golden Bridge–style kundalini yoga classes. A lapsed Parisian runs a French bistro with his *Samaipateña* wife; erstwhile Istanbulites inaugurate the Turkish La Cocina; an Australian couple tends bar at the chilled-out La Bohème on the square. Feng shui architects from Cochabamba and artists from La Paz are also in the house. There's not a single chain store of any kind. Instead, we discover *mingas*, labor-sharing arrangements that weave community interconnection without cash. There's even plans for Transition Tamaysisa, gearing the whole village around carbon neutrality and climate-change resilience.

Five and a half handsome acres, here. Melissa gets out the calculator, and we stay up late trying to figure out how the heck we could afford it. We debate the risk of making a big investment in Bolivia. Most of all, we ask: *Why* would we be buying it? To lock in land for building a house in five years? To pull up stakes and move here soon? Nothing's clear.

After a month in Bolivia, we reach a stalemate in the negotiations with the landowner, who lays down an *oferta final*. Our vacation is about to end. My new semester starts, and Melissa is due back at the UN. Decision time.

The next afternoon, we're at the town's Swiss-run wild animal rescue zoo. The owner, Manuela, has a passion for accepting injured wild animals, or those sadly taken as pets until they became too wild for their owners. She rehabilitates them toward release back into Amboró National Park. About half the animals live outside cages. Nuño — a twenty-pound, orange-haired howler monkey — sits atop my shoulders, his leathery tail around my neck. Nuño's "wife," Cheetah, a smaller, female howler, is on Melissa's shoulders. Amaya is twenty yards away, laughing as she and her friends, Chloe and Lukka, feed papaya to a pair of large tortoises.

"How cool is this?" Melissa says, reaching back to stroke Cheetah.

I feel calm in Tamaysisa. Its giant fern trees rise into blue skies... but so too, under a Slow gaze, does the Freedom Tower in Manhattan. The gleam of the Cuevas waterfalls, just down the river from Tamaysisa, is the Hudson's gleam. Nuño and Cheetah here, Chico the pigeon and Bobby the hawk there. "It's cool. But we're finding this kind of peace in New York."

Melissa flashes a skeptical look. The howler monkey on her shoulder looks equally unconvinced. Cheetah grunts twice, then descends to the ground using Melissa's pregnant belly as a stepping stone.

That night, it's pitch dark in the cozy cabin we've rented for the month. I can hardly make out the banana trees and plump passion fruit hanging on vines beside the back patio, where Melissa and I swing in hammocks. I hear salsa music faintly reverberating from a party some blocks off; frogs peep in the arroyo below the bamboo grove. We still haven't decided whether or not to buy the land. The darkness surrounding us feels foreboding. There's a shadow side to Bolivia. Here we'd be *extranjeros* — foreigners — not citizens who fully belong. There's anti-*extranjero* grumbling in Tamaysisa now, as some locals push back against the changing customs and values brought in by Turks and Thais, Dutch and Danes.

Plus, Bolivia's president Evo Morales has kicked out both the US Drug Enforcement Agency and the US Agency for International Development. An unhappy United States decided to yank all Peace Corps volunteers and rescind Bolivia's tariff preferences. I understand President Morales's position. My own country's "war on drugs" in Bolivia turned out to be a war on the poor. The DEA helped eradicate millions of acres of smallholder coca plants, some of it for a legal local coca-chewing market, bringing violence and upheaval to thousands of indigenous and migrant Bolivians. Morales, himself a Quechua who grew up in a dirt-floor hut, was one of those coca growers. Before winning the presidency in a historic landslide, he ended many of his speeches with: "Death to the Yankees!" Morales is not a Mets fan. He's talking about Melissa and me.

We swing in our hammocks, in the darkness, wrestling with all of this. "Living here would be amazing," Melissa says, "but hard."

"We learned how to do hard in New York."

"You know what?" Melissa says, groping her way upright in the hammock. I can see only the white of her eyes. "All of the messiness in this...It's part of the edge I'm after. If we want fancy drinks with little umbrellas, let's move to the Bahamas."

If you're not on the edge, you're taking up too much space. I feel that. I too want to burrow deeper into the world.

Finally, we come to a decision. A partial one. We'll buy the land. But we'll decide what to do with it later.

Melissa flies back to work, and I stay on to navigate the tricky bureaucracy of Bolivian land tenure. I track down documents, line up in offices, consult with a land rights lawyer. Meanwhile, I teach my first week of NYU classes from Tamaysisa via Skype, with Melissa in the Woolworth Building classroom to assist. Ten days later, I land in JFK and take the subway to West 4th. I thread Cornelia's horse entrance and climb the five flights to our micro. Out of breath, I hand an embossed document to Melissa: the deed to our five and a half acres.

15. THE RIVER

SIX WEEKS LATER, two documents rest on our Ikea collapsible table: the Bolivian land deed and a lease renewal for our Cornelia Street micro-apartment.

Melissa picks up the deed, seeming to test its weight. She places it down and picks up the unsigned lease. She studies it, then looks out the window, still holding it suspended. I follow her gaze to the last of the icicles dripping onto the fire escape.

We're torn. Melissa has a secure post at the UN and has just been offered a raise. I enjoy college teaching, and the 12 x 12 EcoArt project is flourishing. Plus — with the snow almost gone and the tree above Tar Beach covered with sticky buds eager to leaf gloriously out — I'm excited for another music-filled spring in the city.

We've been weighing a move to Bolivia later this year. But the further we lean toward that change, the more we question it. "Just as you've mastered the city at a better speed, you're thinking of *leaving?*" one friend says to us, making an excellent point. Sure, Tamaysisa contains giant fern forests, Inca ruins, and *minga* cooperatives that build community. But even that remote village can't hide from corporate globalization. Miami-worshiping Santa Cruz, a metropolis two hours away, has become one of South America's fastest-growing cities, as high commodity prices and aggressive foreign direct investment crank up its economy — and that city's consumerist values are beginning to spread to Tamaysisa's youth. Whereas before villagers were content to walk, television images have inculcated a "first motorcycle" rite of passage (similar to an American teens' "first car" rite), and Tamaysisa is beginning to roar with unhelmeted sixteen-year-olds on Yamahas. The first smartphones are trickling in, too, and on our last trip we spotted kids zoning out in front of their screens alone instead of playing hide-and-seek in the plaza together.

Melissa suddenly drops the lease she's been holding. She winces and grabs her lower back. I rush to her. On her thin frame, Melissa's nearly full-term pregnant belly seems particularly huge. "Let's get you lying down."

"I've been lying down for two days!" she snaps. "I need some air."

It takes us a full fifteen minutes to descend the five flights, an involuntary Slow thrust on us by a flaring up of Melissa's sciatic nerve, a late-pregnancy condition where the fetus pushes against one of the body's biggest nerves. Each step she takes shoots searing pain up her left side and through her lumbar. Sweating in my wool coat, I act as a crutch. At last, we shuffle, arms locked, through the horse entrance gate, inch past brash Papaya Dog, and enter the southwest corner of Washington

Square Park. Though the musicians still hibernate, the first kelly-green daffodil shoots are pushing up through the thawing soil.

We hobble toward Prodigy. What's usually a five-minute walk takes nearly an hour. *Heel-toe. Heel-toe.* I try to savor each footfall. I feel useful, holding up my wife. I imagine us as an eighty-year-old Greenwich Village couple, shuffling through these same streets. We receive several impatient glares — we're hindering the blaze of pedestrians into offices and subway tunnels. I notice Melissa holding a Slow City calm; she points out a third-story gargoyle. I follow her lead and squint, taxi-top ads become lovely impressionist blurs. On MacDougal Street, I stop to appreciate a dust mote afloat, remembering Amaya, as a baby, noticing every tiny detail like that. My gaze loosens from the dust and falls upon the sleek strong body of the Freedom Tower. I follow its line into the glorious bowl of blue, the more-than-human that's always available; a waning moon rises in the east. A slightly indignant heat is starting to rise in me. I do not want to leave New York.

What had been our Manhattan experiment has become our life. Now that an expiration date threatens that life, I cling tight to it. That's *my* Freedom Tower. My moonrise. My dust mote.

The West Village is our neighborhood, the Hudson is our river. These subways and buses belong to us, and I don't want to leave New York, despite the filthy gum wads worn into the sidewalk at my feet, despite the chintzy plastic *Village Voice* kiosks, despite the predatory traffic and helicopters — and the constant pedicure come-ons and Brazilian-threading-and-waxing-tattoos-art-films-sample-sales-crack-pedaling disarray. Despite all of this — partly because of it — I do not want to leave New York. My Irish grandfather didn't brave an ocean to Ellis Island so that I would one day abandon New York City for a village in Bolivia. I love Pearl's scallops, Small Liberia's palm butter, Murray's bagels; I love the Chinese decorative arts, the High Line, fire-lit Jones Street jazz. I love flashing my NYU ID at the Bobst Library, idling with Bruce and the Jam under the arch, riding a yellow Iverson bike along the Hudson. I love Tar Beach, our micro-apartment, and the million marvels surrounding it, and I'm not going to give that all up for a village in Bolivia.

In Prodigy, over coffee, we watch the first leaves budding on the tree beside Unoppressive, Non-Imperialist Bargain Books. I'm drained by inner turmoil over the decision. Melissa says: "What do we do?"

I RETREAT TO BEAR MOUNTAIN on the Shortline bus. My mother suggests it, saying I need "discernment" time about this big decision. She did something similar in 1969. Then, she was discerning whether to remove her Catholic nun's habit after over a decade as Sister Veronica, become Ann once again, and marry my father, a former priest. Should she break her vows and take new ones?

The Village or a village? I write this in my notebook. Of course, it's a decision that Melissa and I have to make together, but as she delves into an intense week of work, I take this chance to get some clarity for myself, walking with this question through Doodletown and along the Appalachian Trail, slippery with snowmelt and mud. I sit with the question in my slope-ceilinged room on the top floor of Bear Mountain Inn, and it flows into an evening of writing and prepping my

Thursday class. Every once in a while I get up from my laptop and gaze out at Hessian Lake through the dormer window. The world looks empty. Midweek, off-season, it seems I'm the only guest. I squint out into the forest beyond the moonlit lake, a schist outcrop looking like a ruined farmhouse.

At 8 PM I hear a sudden knock at the door. I seize up. I don't know anybody here.

Then, a second, more-hesitant knock. I open the door. It's the blonde, middle-aged receptionist who checked me in. She holds out a second room key for me. She's sorry to disturb me, but she forgot to give it to me. It seems odd, since I checked in alone, and I tell her that.

"Then I suppose you won't be needing it. I'm Janet." She extends a confident hand, gives me an extra-firm shake. Her posture is arrow-straight, her attractive cheekbones high. "By the way," she asks, "are you a writer?"

I stiffen a bit — I've come for seclusion, not conversation — and nod.

"Oh, I thought so. You just...*seemed* like one. I want to write a book, and I'm looking for someone to help me."

"What about?" I ask. Her presence — incongruent, unexpected — suddenly feels natural. Part of living the improvisation of Slow is embracing the unforeseen as normal.

"My ex-husband," she says. "We were divorced six months ago. He's a four-star general and a top army commander in Europe. Eleventh in GPA at West Point, 1986. It turns out that, after twenty-five years in the service, he's suddenly committing adultery, embezzling, and all sorts of other crimes. And guess what? I'm the one who turned him in."

A mischievous and charming smile spreads across Janet's

face. She places her hands on the tight belt accenting her waist. "He's been court-martialed. Had an Iraqi mistress, a young thing. He took her on staff, spent eighty thousand of *your* tax dollars to bring her around the world as an interpreter, staying in fancy hotels. She *wasn't* an interpreter."

The story gets worse. Multiple mistresses; he lashes back and sues Janet under the Hague Act; counter-lawsuits. Even David Petraeus and his adultery are woven in. "Those lavish dinners with David and Holly Petraeus..." she says, her smile long evaporated. Pain, *pain,* seems to prick every part of her; with each detail, she feels more like a saguaro cactus with the spines pointing in.

I lay a hand on her shoulder. Tell her how sorry I am. She's bitter, saying how even though she "got him court-martialed," it was just cosmetic; he kept his benefits. "The military's old boys' club protects its own, and meanwhile my alimony is chickenfeed." I nod, listen, offer sympathetic words. Her posture slumps; she spills out how she nearly lost custody of her son to her ex-husband, how the expensive lawsuits he laid on her left her penniless. "That's why I'm a receptionist now."

Silence. She looks down at her hands. It's begun raining outside; I hear it on the windowsill behind me. We've been standing in the doorway for twenty minutes, and it suddenly feels awkward, too intimate. I take in her scrupulously ironed clothes, the razor-straight bangs across her forehead, and picture her as wife of a powerful US general entertaining the Petraeuses, before a drone flew over her life.

THE NEXT AFTERNOON, the Indian Head nuclear alarm sounds. I cover my ears but don't run this time. I remain planted on the highest boulder over a wind-blown Hessian Lake. Cars barrel by on the highway, across the lake, beyond the leafless trees. The siren penetrates me, my fingers doing little to dampen it, so I lean into the noise. Lean on what is.

Finally, it stops. *This was a test*, announces the cyborg, the metallic voice now almost a fixture of Bear Mountain for me. A train horn sounds. Two figures work their way through the mud, southbound on the Appalachian Trail, their packs wrapped in rain covers. Up the mountain, pitch the tent, blaze up the cook stove, eat ramen, curl up in a down sleeping bag. Repeat. Repeat, monastically, for months, maybe. I think back to Janet, at the front desk this morning, bright-eyed today, with none of yesterday's bitterness, her back snapped to erect.

Now, on this water-slicked boulder, I consider some facts: Janet has a sixteen-year-old son ("Who *I* got to keep. He lives with *me*."). Her son's football team made it to the regionals this year and were just a field goal away from the state finals. There are only 423 people in her son's high school, so that's impressive. There are other facts: I've witnessed the seasons change under Bear Mountain, a place I didn't know existed until we moved from Queens to Manhattan. Here, I've seen jade forest so thick that it hid the eight lanes of highway just beyond; then autumn's orange, red, and yellow; winter's denuded branches over Hessian Lake, crowned with ice. More facts: The rock on which I stand is schist, finely interleaved with feldspar and quartz. The loamy humus in front of me sprouts dogwoods that evolved from a huge adaptive radiation that created Earth's first trees in Devonian times, 360 million years ago. But facts are a flimsy sieve with which to sift for truth, since facts are infinite. I drop out of my intellect, slowly inhabiting flesh, the second chakra, which I learned about in Amanbir's class. Our lower spinal cords contain as many firing synapses as the brain. "The second brain," as some scientists term it, the bottom of our nervous system at the base of the spine. It's an intelligence center long called intuition or the "gut feeling."

The Village or a village? I ask from my gut. Though I haven't been walking my question in a straight line, something about Bear Mountain, and the encounter with Janet, obliquely illuminates it. I question the drama — adultery, divorce, warfare, embezzlement — that has become almost normal. It fills the news, along with up-to-the-minute gory violence and the military's next target. Sensation grows and you wonder which is feeding which: people's actions creating the news or news creating their actions? A thousand vehicles fly southbound beyond Hessian Lake, toward Manhattan. More still cross the Bear Mountain Bridge, which straddles the Hudson River before me, carrying additional cars that race to the city. From the top of the bridge's arch droops a mammoth American flag. Fifty feet long, its effervescent red, white, and blue smolder in fabric. I *should* want to cross this flawless bridge and take a First World highway to Manhattan. But I'm dreaming of other bridges to cross as I watch the flag's colors weaken and the Hudson's sparkle drain to black.

MELISSA'S TRAIN LEAVES IN AN HOUR. We're standing, for the last time together, atop Tar Beach.

The courtyard tree's first leaves have opened into a lime-green patina above our heads. My eye scans the fire escapes for baby mourning doves. Though I spot a nest, no squeakers are audible yet.

Below our feet, our micro-apartment is nearly as bare as it was when we first viewed it almost a year back. The furniture is mostly gone. In the kitchen, there's just one fork, one spoon, and one knife beside a single cup and plate. A single sleeping bag, the one I used in the Harriman lean-to, is unfurled before the swept-clean fireplace. Beside the fireplace, a few final boxes marked "Goodwill" and "Bolivia."

Melissa, accompanied by her father, will ride the south-bound Amtrak to North Carolina today, to Chapel Hill, where my parents live and where we will give birth. We didn't find the kind of birthing center we wanted in New York, and we had no room to host family in our micro — and we awoke to the fact that, indeed, we would need support before and after the birth. Since my parents' town has a simple, attractive birthing center staffed by midwives — we decided to leave New York sooner than expected.

"The excitement I feel right now…" Melissa says. "It reminds me of the Durkheim quote you use in your class. About how, in society, we can have what we want, but not *want* what we want."

The sun cracks through the Sixth Avenue buildings. We let it warm our faces. I ask her what she means.

"By becoming gypsies just when the demographic of 'new parents' is told to nest, we're crushing another box."

I'm not quite as confident as Melissa about our plan: First, giving birth in North Carolina at a birthing center we love, but which lacks doctors and high-tech equipment. Then, taking our two-month-old Squeaker on a family-and-friends tour across America. Finally, when she's six months old, migrate south to construct an eco-house on our acres — to revillage in Tamaysisa.

The single spoon, fork, and knife in the kitchen — they're mine. I will stay on for another week to teach and tie up some loose ends at the World Policy Institute. I'll have to commute from North Carolina back to New York three times to wrap up the semester. I worry a bit that, when you crush boxes, what's still inside gets smashed up, too.

"WE NEED TO GO!" I shout across the lawn to Melissa's father. He runs for his car keys as I help Melissa, who is bent over and letting out a deep long moan. Her contractions have suddenly dropped to under three minutes apart and her legs and sandals are soaked. Her water just broke.

In the car, she's whimpering, then gritting teeth and crying out as each contraction hits. We arrive at the North Carolina

Birth and Wellness Center and stagger inside. It's an ordinary-looking kitchen and living room, not a clinic. The midwife helps us into a beautiful room, like one at home — but one that lacks comforting emergency equipment.

An hour passes, then two, as Melissa pushes, first on the bed, and then, because it's more comfortable for her, in a tub of warm water. I'm calmed by the assurance of the nurse and the midwife accompanying us. The sun sets through the window, and the pair of red cardinals that have been singing to us fly off.

My parents join hers in the dining room, and the four of them sip wine and eat the cooked meal my mom brought along. I hear their muffled laughter in the gaps between Melissa's groans and shrieks in the tub. It's dark out the window. The midwife turns out the lights, and I light candles. The nurse floats a flashlight sealed in a Ziploc bag on the water. Melissa's beautiful face illuminates in the flicker of candles and by the flashlight bobbing on the water.

I become anxious again. Melissa pushes and pushes. Nothing. It's taking too long.

I get up from where I kneel by the tub and play Snatam Kaur's mantras on the CD player, the same music we heard in Amanbir's class at Golden Bridge in Manhattan.

Sat Nam, she sings, over and over. *Sat Nam*: My path is truth. I realize Melissa is mirroring the mantra in slow drawn-out guttural sounds. The primal sounds of a mother about to bring a new life into the world.

I kneel again beside Melissa. She grips my arm. I notice something wrong in the illuminated water. Our baby's been crowning for a half hour, but now, in the dim light, I'm certain I see a tiny eye. A tiny nose.

She's too small.

My heart ticks faster. I'm imagining a pint-sized two-pounder, when, all at once, after a final loud grand push, our baby — Clea Luz — is born into the water.

The midwife guides her to Melissa's chest, where she sits in all her purple grandeur, not yet oxygenated to have the pearly pink complexion we might expect. Clea is large and healthy. Melissa cries out in a loud whisper: "She's a miracle!"

My hands shake. The midwife hands me surgical scissors. I know what I'm to do. I steady my hands and cut the umbilical cord clean through.

They tie Clea's cord, and while they're attending to Melissa, they pass my daughter to me. Eight pounds of moist, weeping love on my bare chest. She's got my red hair. Melissa's green-blue eyes. After an hour, I open the door. The four grandparents' hopeful eyes lock into mine. Reverently, they enter the candlelit room to meet their grandchild.

THE NOMADIC MONTHS AFTER CLEA'S BIRTH flow like the Hudson. For two months, we rent in a cohousing community near my parents; there, with all four grandparents present, we bury Clea's placenta in the community's loblolly pine grove. Then six weeks at Melissa's adobe-style home in Santa Fe, where Clea is blessed by the minister on the altar of her grandparents' Episcopalian church. A month in my sister's solar dome in Vermont, swimming in creeks, picking blueberries, and harvesting vegetables from the garden. A month in Melissa's family's clapboard summerhouse on the Cape, carrying the growing Clea in her sling through Barnstable Harbor's salt marshes as the tide slurps in and out.

There are challenges: packing and unpacking, adjusting to others' rhythms, the baby wailing at 3 in the morning. I struggle to fit my four-day workweek of writing and remote World Policy Institute project management into our family rhythm. But, on the whole, our experiment with gypsy Slow Parenting invigorates. We don't rush into full-time work. We don't buy anything new for Clea (relying on hand-me-downs or thrift shops). We take back our time, give it to Clea, and watch how her smiles bring joy to the myriad people on the road.

En route from Santa Fe to Vermont, we swing through New York for the launch of the 12 x 12 at the Queens Botanical Gardens. It's dreamlike, walking with my parents, Melissa, and a swaddled Clea toward a tiny dot at the center of the gardens' thirty-nine acres. As we cross the lawn, the dot becomes a box. It's exquisitely surreal. In New York City, I'm suddenly walking through the door of the off-grid cabin I lived in on No Name Creek and wrote about in *Twelve by Twelve*. This spawned cabin is different; its creators have midwifed art. A 12 x 12 eco-house with retracting walls, a solar roof, and a resident artist, now busy painting burlap sacks inside as she interacts with visitors about genetically modified seeds. Something is painted on the wall. It reads: "What's *your* 12 x 12?"

During the party, my mother comes over and hugs me, enthusing: "This is wonderful!" We trade smiles. Our migration includes family. She and my dad will visit us in Bolivia, for Amaya's birthday, and my sister and her family of five are coming down, too — for six months, to expose their four-, seven-, and ten-year-old children to a Slower culture. They'll attend Tamaysisa's fledgling alternative school, Flor de Montana, based on Andean ecological stewardship.

Melissa and I want to assist with the emerging Transition Tamaysisa — bringing the town into the global Transition movement for sustainable local economies. We'll use the World Policy Institute's network to help measure Tamaysisa's happiness levels, confirming initial evidence that, in a preconsumerist village like Tamaysisa that uses very little fossil fuels per capita, happiness levels equal to those in the West can be achieved on one-fifth its GDP.

The patio around us is thronged with entrepreneurs and academics, policy makers and students. They coo over baby Clea and weave through the 12 x 12, sipping drinks. I feel high. There's a sense of shifting paradigms. Ripples. The pebble: a physician, Jackie Benton, who moves off-grid to a 12 x 12 to lower her carbon footprint. I meet her, live in her place, write about it. Then, artists and architects create this. *Soul flares*. And next?

I never see the installation again. Some twenty thousand others do, at the botanical gardens and, after, when the 12 x 12 moves to First Park in Greenwich Village — even more when other 12 x 12s sprout on college campuses in the coming year. Ripples. Create, let go.

BEFORE LEAVING NEW YORK, I take the A train to West 4th Street. My favorite student, JT, wants to say good-bye, so I suggest we meet under the Washington Square Arch.

It's hot and humid. Beneath the park's now lush tree canopy a half dozen musical acts perform, including Bruce and the Jam. I stand on the edge of the Jam, clapping to Marvin Gaye's "What's Going On?" *We've got to find a way to bring some lovin' here today!* Between riffs, Bruce nods to me and shrugs,

Soul flares

as if to ask, "Where you been?" Beyond the Jam, people feed pigeons. Where William the Pigeon Guy always used to stand, two attractive young women have migrated in and are feeding pigeons almonds from their mouths — and one beige bird is unmistakably Chico. A red-tailed hawk circles above, eyeing its terrain for dove and pigeon steaks. I talk to a man photographing the hawk, and he says it's not Bobby but rather "somebody new." The new hawk rides a thermal over the arch, and I read the single quote engraved in huge letters at the very top of the arch. It's from George Washington: "Let us raise a standard to which the wise and the honest can repair. The event is in the hands of God."

I've read the quote many times. While daydreaming on the lawn, while walking back from Golden Bridge to Cornelia Street, and — most often — while listening, like now, to the Jam. I've never quite understood our first president's words. But now, Bruce nailing a wild, contained riff, it's a revelation. *Let us raise a standard*...A jazz standard. A Slow standard. A standard that's unreasonable...*to which the wise and the honest can repair.* We're broken. But through that fresh standard we repair ourselves, heal our culture. *The event is in the hands of God.* Then let go.

Washington wasn't trying to be Slow. But his words, emblazoned over my head in Greenwich Village all year long, encapsulate much of what I've learned.

"Professor!"

JT. He joins me. We listen to Bruce for a while, and then we stroll together. I can't believe how much JT has changed from our first classes a year back. From simplistic statements like "But poor countries need to develop like us, right?" he's

Bolivia – Living Well

become so much more nuanced about how power shapes discourse, colonizes our words. Now he's got his own inventive thinking about the place of humans in a finite biosphere.

"I want to take your new course," he says, referring to my two-week Bolivia Field Intensive. I'll bring NYU graduate students to La Paz, Santa Cruz, and Tamaysisa to study Living Well — Bolivia's new riff on gross national happiness — and its evolving Law of Mother Earth, which grants the planet rights, including the right to "not have its physical processes destroyed by mega-infrastructure projects."

Before we part, I hand something to JT. It's the leather-bound Bolivian notebook I've toted along all year. He flips past *Is idleness treason?*, a sketch of the Natural City, and *What's food to you?* Then he comes to the hundred pages at the end. They're blank. "Write on them, paint them, or burn them," I tell JT, "but always walk questioning."

We hug farewell, and I head down to the Hudson alone.

On the tip of Pier 45, I gaze down the Hudson to a distant Freedom Tower raging in late-afternoon sunlight. As a child I'd marvel at the World Trade Center from the 83rd Place hill in Queens, just above Nana and Pop's. And I remember standing directly beneath the Twin Towers with my parents one day and feeling so inconsequential next to them. A few months back, I watched a hundred workers in hard hats, pointing phones to the sky, filming the finale of their toils — the raising of the Freedom Tower's spire, which made the building 1776 feet high. As the spire went up, I began to grasp that trauma is assimilated, that we can reimagine afresh. Sandy's havoc, too, is partly absorbed. Though Pier 45's benches remain smashed, the Bedouin tent is mended. The crystal wavelets between Hoboken and me are candles set afloat by monks.

My gaze lengthens to where the Hudson opens into New York Harbor, and then into the Atlantic. Out there soars a plane, like the one that will carry us to Amaya. My heart thrums at the thought of our reunion, of living near my daughter. Amaya is elated to meet her baby sister, Clea. "Daddy, I'm shaking with joy," she told me on the phone the other day. And a Bolivian eco-architect friend has sent us initial sketches of our home, to be made of adobe from our land. Large passive solar windows. Encircled by permaculture gardens, Tamaysisa's climate allowing temperate apples and peaches, tropical kiwis and papayas. One side of our home's slow curving walls will face outward, over the clay roofs of the pueblo, and the other will gaze quietly inward toward our *guaparu* groves and a trickle of creek that flows to the Piraí to the Amazon, into the great Atlantic. And the rivers are one.

Still, how tricky to tear myself from my favorite river, as it splashes the pylons underfoot. The tango dancers arrive and pull on polished shoes, and the sound of nineteenth-century bandolon mixes with the tinkling of crabbing bells on an old Chinese man's pole tips. We nod to each other; we've been silent partners-in-idleness on Pier 45 this year. Then I think with fondness of another immigrant, my grandfather, and of how lavishly big-hearted this city is, and how mercurial. The hirsute Chinese man, leaving five crabbing-poles untended, attaches a large silver sea-bass lure — in the shape of a minnow — onto a surf-casting rod and prepares to cast.

There's a vast pause. The rod's weight suspended over his

shoulder, the fisher closes his eyes, as if searching within himself for the location of fish in the Hudson. A hundred traffic lights on the West Side Highway flip to red. There's no aircraft above. Heads flick to promenade; the tango stops between songs. My monkey-mind, too, has stopped. I'm not thinking of Bruce's riffs or Anastasia's rooftop artichokes. I'm neither sunk to the bleak bottom of the Bronx River nor risen to the feral crest of a Rockaway wave. I watch a man gather musculature into a rod's heavy bend. When his arms finally spring forward and the lure's silver explodes, I attend to a skyward streak of a minnow alone. And that, after so many generous teachers and tools revealed, feels like the richest harvest of the city slow: a minnow flashing into the Freedom Tower's blaze.

ACKNOWLEDGMENTS

THE IDEAS IN *New Slow City* bubbled up from fifteen years of exploring the Leisure Ethic in Europe, Africa, Latin America, and North America. I thank the innumerable people and communities around the globe who have fed these pages.

Thank you to John de Graaf, Vicki Robin, David Abram, and Louisa Putnam for your inspiring ideas and exchanges, and also to Tom Hodgkinson (for ideas in chapter 2), and Carl Honoré (for ideas in chapter 3). I am grateful to my bright and enthusiastic New York University students. Much appreciation to Amanbir, Harinam, and the other quality teachers at Golden Bridge NYC.

Thank you, Eric Morrissey and Lucy Flood, for your creativity in helping shape this book.

I am grateful to the World Policy Institute's president, Michele Wucker, and the director of development, Kate Maloff, for your strong support.

New World Library's extraordinary team has helped make this book go live. A special thank you to Jason Gardner, my editor, as well as Monique Muhlenkamp, Munro Magruder, Ami Parkerson, and Jonathan Wichmann. Copyeditor Jeff Campbell, as always, is fantastic. Thank you to my agent, Michael Bourret of Dystel and Goderich.

For retreat space during this book's writing, I am grateful to John and Lucy Draper (Santa Fe and Cape Cod), Phil and Jeanie Kithil (Santa Fe), Pieter and Marga at La Vispera organic farm (Bolivia), Nancy Romer and Lew Friedman (Park Slope), Kate and Andy Hilton (New Hampshire), and these generous Vermonters for opening up their quiet homes: my sister, Amy, and brother-in-law, Andrew; Cath and Earnie; Robin and Greg; Eve and David; and Jon-by-the-Winooski.

Thank you to my mother and father for your love and encouragement, a foundation from which all the adventures and ideas have sprung. And also to my late grandparents, Nana and Pop, for starting the Victory Garden and carving out a home for our family in the big city, even before it hit high speed.

Thank you, Amaya and Clea, for your love, hugs, and "crazy hour" fun.

Above all, my gratitude to Melissa — skilled editor, eternal optimist, love of my life.

ABOUT THE AUTHOR

WILLIAM POWERS has worked for two decades in development aid and conservation in Latin America, Africa, and North America. From 2002 to 2004 he managed the community components of a project in the Bolivian Amazon that won a 2003 prize for environmental innovation from Harvard's John F. Kennedy School of Government. His essays and commentaries on global issues have appeared in the *New York Times* and the *International Herald Tribune* and on National Public Radio's *Fresh Air*. Powers has worked at the World Bank and holds international relations degrees from Brown and Georgetown. A third-generation New Yorker, Powers has also spent two decades exploring the American culture of speed and its alternatives in some fifty countries around the world. He has covered the subject in his four books and written about it in the *Washington Post* and the *Atlantic*. Powers is a senior fellow at the World Policy Institute and an adjunct faculty member at New York University. His website is www.williampowersbooks.com.

ALSO BY WILLIAM POWERS

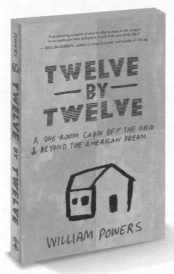

"How much is enough? And what is really important? These are questions that William Powers runs into again and again in his time off the grid in the U.S. and overseas, but his humble and contemplative memoir handles them with freshness and honesty, recognizing that sometimes asking the questions is more important than finding the 'right' answers."

— **Lester R. Brown, president of Earth Policy Institute and author of *Plan B 4.0: Mobilizing to Save Civilization***

"The beauty of the book lies in Powers' generous intimacy.... *Twelve by Twelve* makes a huge bow to Thoreau, but it is...far more spiritual.... We watch Powers rethink his entire approach; we watch him relax into himself, become himself, carve himself out of a dream that was not his own." — *Los Angeles Times*

"A penetrating account of what it's like to move to the margins in our particular time and place. It will make you think, hard."
— **Bill McKibben, author of *Deep Economy* and founder of 350.org**